Treasures
from the
'30s

Cheerful Quilts
with Vintage Appeal

NANCY MAHONEY

Martingale®
& COMPANY

ACKNOWLEDGMENTS

A very special thanks to:

✶ First and foremost, to Tom Reichert for his never-ending support and encouragement. He's the best!

✶ The delightful people at Martingale & Company; this team of dedicated women and men are always a joy to work with! Thank you for making this book possible.

✶ Nannette Moore and Kelly Wise, machine quilters extraordinaire. Their talent and imaginative quilting breathed life into these quilts.

✶ Kathy, Kelly, Denise, Jan, Melanie, and everyone at the Sew and Quilt Shop in Bunnell, Florida—a wonderful bunch of gals!

✶ The Memory Makers Quilt Guild—a fantastic group of women, whose enthusiastic oohs and aahs encourage me to try new things.

✶ The following companies who generously provided so many great products: P&B Textiles, whose lovely fabrics created so many of the quilts; Sulky® for threads and adhesives; Fairfield for their terrific batting; Prym Dritz for their rulers and other exceptional products; and the Warm Company for their outstanding fusible web products.

Treasures from the '30s: Cheerful Quilts with Vintage Appeal
© 2010 by Nancy Mahoney

That Patchwork Place® is an imprint
of Martingale & Company®.

Martingale & Company
20205 144th Ave. NE
Woodinville, WA 98072-8478 USA
www.martingale-pub.com

Printed in China
15 14 13 12 11 10   9 8 7 6 5 4 3 2 1

Library of Congress Cataloging-in-Publication Data is available upon request.

ISBN: 978-1-60468-004-1

MISSION STATEMENT

*Dedicated to providing quality products
and service to inspire creativity.*

CREDITS

President & CEO: Tom Wierzbicki

Editor in Chief: Mary V. Green

Managing Editor: Tina Cook

Developmental Editor: Karen Costello Soltys

Technical Editor: Ursula Reikes

Copy Editor: Marcy Heffernan

Design Director: Stan Green

Production Manager: Regina Girard

Illustrator: Laurel Strand

Cover & Text Designer: Regina Girard

Photographer: Brent Kane

Contents

THE QUILTS

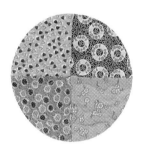

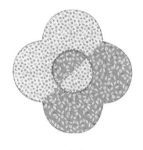

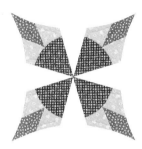

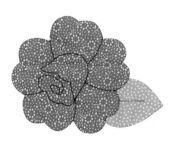

Introduction

When I started quilting, I was a purist. I wanted to continue the art of quilting much as our grandmothers and great-grandmothers did. (Actually, my grandmother wasn't a quilter!) Now 25+ years later, I'm a realist. There are too many quilts that I want to make, and too little time. That's one reason I enjoy collecting vintage quilts; I can own a beautiful patchwork or appliquéd quilt without having to make it! It's awe inspiring to know that I share the same passion for quilting as quilters from the past, and I appreciate the struggles those quilters went through to make beautiful quilts. Quilts from the 1930s are a legacy, bearing witness to a quiet movement toward social progress.

During the thirties and early forties, times were hard and "waste not, want not" was a common mantra. Bragging rights were often based on the clever use of a discarded item. Women prided themselves on their resolve to make do with less. The national quilt revival of the 1930s provided many with a creative way to do just that. Beyond creating something practical, quilting also provided a means for women to contribute to the household's shrinking income. Many women saw an increasing demand for their needle arts and started their own home-based businesses, enjoying success and even financial independence.

Just as quilters today embrace new products and techniques, so did the women of yesteryear. In the early 1900s, electrically powered sewing machines were widely used and could be purchased on an installment plan. Despite the financial limits of the thirties, new patterns and quilting aids continued to be advertised. Quilting products were a major industry, and advertisers sold all sorts of labor-saving devices, from iron-on quilting patterns to precut fabric for so-called "kit" quilts.

By 1934 most metropolitan newspapers featured articles on quiltmaking, with the quilt article as the most popular Sunday feature. Some newspapers featured a quilt block with templates that could be clipped and saved; others featured a block drawing and offered a full-sized pattern for 10¢ or 15¢. I'm so thankful these patterns were collected and cherished by quilters.

As a twenty-first-century quilter, I often feel I have a foot in two centuries. I love antiques, and almost anything vintage. My nineteenth-century oak roll-top desk was allegedly owned by a magician. I adore its simple, solid style with all the little drawers and cubbyholes. It's a wonderful workspace for my laptop, and I can sit there for hours in my ergonomically designed chair. I also love using my computerized sewing

machine and rotary cutting tools to make quilts using block designs from the '30s.

For this book, I've selected eight patterns from my collection of '30s quilt patterns. As in my other two books, *Quilt Revival* (Martingale & Company, 2006) and *Appliqué Quilt Revival* (Martingale & Company, 2008), the projects on these pages are scrappy in style, constructed with 1930s reproduction fabrics, but they make use of updated appliqué and piecing techniques. Some of the projects are a bit more challenging, but you'll also find projects for the confident beginner. If you're a less-experienced quilter, dive in and try something new! The designs may look complicated, but they really aren't.

One valuable lesson I learned many years ago, while working in a tailoring shop, applies to quilting (and life in general): When faced with a difficult or complicated task, don't dwell on how much there is to be done, take it one step at a time and before you know it, the job will be finished.

And there you have it, but there's one more thing I want to share with you before getting to the really important stuff—the quilts! As I was writing this book, I thought it would be fun to research 1930 to 1939. I became totally fascinated with all of the events that took place during that decade. We think of the thirties as being hard and depressing, but there were also wonderful, amazing things that happened, and I wanted to share some of the good times with you as well.

Dateline–1930

* First year of the Great Depression

* Herbert Hoover is President of the United States

* A new planet beyond Neptune is discovered and named "Pluto"

* The Chrysler Building in New York City officially opens to the public

* Sliced bread goes on sale in England for the first time

* Stamps are 2¢

* "Blondie" comic strip by Chic Young begins

* Books released include *As I Lay Dying* by William Faulkner and *The Maltese Falcon* by Dashiell Hammett

* Academy Award winner for Best Picture of 1930 is *All Quiet on the Western Front*

In this section, you'll find the piecing and appliqué techniques that I used to complete the quilts in this book. Feel free to use your own methods or use this section as a guide for the special techniques used in the quilt you're making.

ROTARY CUTTING

All of the projects in this book are designed for rotary cutting and are easily pieced by machine. Use your rotary cutter to cut block backgrounds and borders as well as the patchwork strips and pieces in your project. All rotary-cutting measurements include ¼"-wide seam allowances. Basic rotary-cutting tools include a rotary cutter, an 18" x 24" cutting mat, a 6" Bias Square® ruler, and a 6" x 24" acrylic ruler. You'll be able to make all of the projects in this book with these tools. I use the 6" Bias Square for making cleanup cuts and for crosscutting squares.

Rotary cutting squares, rectangles, and other shapes begins with cutting accurate strips. Note that the following rotary-cutting instructions are written for right-handers; reverse the instructions if you're left-handed.

Begin by pressing the fabric, and then folding it in half with the selvages together. Place the fabric on your cutting mat with the folded edge nearest to your body. To make a cleanup cut, align the Bias Square ruler with the fold of the fabric and place a 6" x 24" ruler to the left so that the raw edges of the fabric are covered.

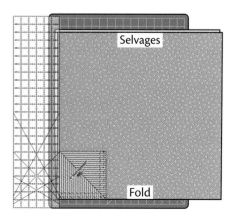

Remove the Bias Square ruler and make a rotary cut along the right side of the long ruler. Remove the long ruler and gently remove the waste strip. This is known as a cleanup cut.

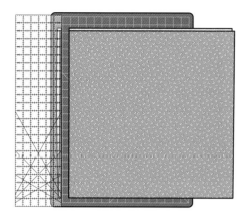

To cut strips, align the desired width measurement on the ruler with the cut edge of the fabric and carefully cut the strip. After cutting three or four strips, realign the Bias Square ruler along the fold and make a new cleanup cut.

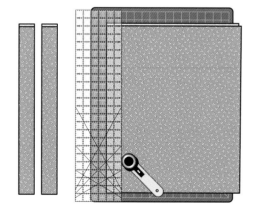

To cut squares and rectangles, cut strips in the desired widths. Cut the selvage ends off the strip in the same way that you made the cleanup cut. Align the required measurement on the ruler with the left edge of the strip and cut a square or rectangle. Continue cutting until you have the required number of pieces.

APPLIQUÉ TECHNIQUES

There are many ways to appliqué—both by hand and by machine. Each method uses different techniques. Before starting an appliqué project, you can choose which method is best for a particular project. If you're making a special heirloom quilt, you may want to use a hand appliqué method. If, however, you're making a quilt that will receive hard wear, machine appliqué is often the best and most efficient choice. Or you may find you'll want to use a combination of methods or techniques.

Cutting Background Fabric

All of the appliqué patterns in this book are printed full size. Because appliqué blocks tend to become slightly distorted and fray during stitching, for most projects you'll be cutting the block backgrounds 1" larger than the finished size and trimming them to the correct size after completing the appliqué. For instance, for a 9" finished block, normally the background fabric would be cut 9½" x 9½" to allow for ¼" seam allowance on all sides. For appliqué, the block background is cut 10" x 10", and then trimmed to 9½" x 9½". Use a rotary cutter, mat, and acrylic ruler to accurately cut the blocks.

Once you've cut your block backgrounds, mark the center of each piece by folding it in half vertically and horizontally; then lightly finger-press to create center-lines.

Making Appliqué Templates

Since you'll be making more than one of each appliqué piece, you'll find it handy to make a plastic template for each pattern piece. Templates made from clear or frosted plastic are durable and accurate, and because you can see through the plastic, you can easily trace the shapes from the patterns. You can trace the pieces of each appliqué design directly from the pattern to create the templates you'll need. Seam allowances are not included on templates for appliqué pieces. Prepare your templates accurately to ensure the best results. *Be sure to use heat-resistant template plastic when making templates that will be used for the starch appliqué technique described on page 8.*

To make the templates, place template plastic over each pattern piece and trace with a fine-line permanent marker, making sure to trace the lines exactly. Do not mark a seam allowance, unless a seam allowance is included in the pattern piece. Use utility scissors to cut out the templates, cutting exactly on the drawn lines. Write the block name and pattern number on the template. This is the right side of the template. You need only one plastic template for each different pattern piece.

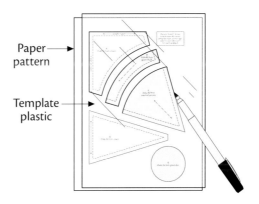

Paper pattern

Template plastic

Appliqué Patterns

Only one appliqué pattern in this book has been drawn reversed for starch appliqué and fusible appliqué. If you're using a hand appliqué technique, such as needle-turn appliqué, or if you're making a placement guide, you'll need to make a reversed, or mirror, image of the rose pattern on page 55. The rest of the appliqué patterns are symmetrical and don't need to be reversed.

To make a plastic template for needle-turn appliqué, simply trace the pattern, and then turn your template over and mark that as the right side.

To make a reverse image for a placement guide, trace the entire appliqué pattern onto a piece of paper; then place the paper on a light box or against a bright window, with the traced side toward the light. Trace the shape onto the back of the paper using a black permanent pen.

Appliqué Placement

An easy way to place the appliqué pieces on the block background is to make and use a placement guide underneath the background piece. To make a placement guide, trace the pattern onto a piece of paper.

I also like to draw the finished block size around the pattern. This is helpful when the edges of appliqué pieces are sewn into the seam later. Do this by placing a square ruler over the pattern with the midpoint of the block over the center point marked on the patterns. Trace two sides of the ruler, rotate the paper, reposition the ruler, and draw the other two sides.

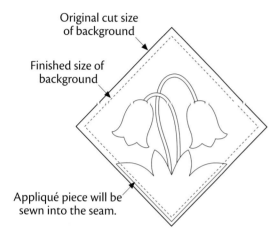

Original cut size of background

Finished size of background

Appliqué piece will be sewn into the seam.

Lay the placement guide on a table or your ironing board, and lay the background piece over it. Carefully match the center marks and pin in place. Position the appliqués on the background, following the alphabetical order marked on the pattern. If you find it difficult to see your design through the background fabric, you can use a light box.

Starch Appliqué

This appliqué technique uses a template as a base to make a smooth, curved edge on an appliqué shape and is similar to freezer-paper appliqué, except you're using heat-resistant template plastic instead of freezer paper.

For this method you'll need a can of spray starch, a small cup, and a small (¼") foam pounce or cotton swab. Using starch saves time when preparing the pieces for appliqué, and unlike the glue-stick method, you don't need to soak the fabrics in water to remove the starch.

With this method you can prepare all the pieces for the block and preview them before stitching. The pieces can be stitched by hand or machine.

1. Using heat-resistant template plastic, make one template of each appliqué shape, referring to "Making Appliqué Templates" on page 7.

2. Place each template right side up on the wrong side of the chosen fabric. Trace around the template using a pencil. Cut out the shape, adding a ³⁄₁₆"-wide seam allowance all around.

Skip the Tracing

Instead of tracing around the template, place a piece of double-stick tape on the wrong side of the template. The tape will hold the template in place as you cut out the fabric shape *and* as you press the edges over the template.

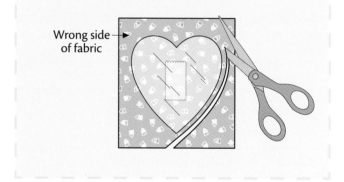

Wrong side of fabric

3. Place the appliqué shape flat, with the wrong side up, on your ironing board. Center the plastic template, right side up, on the wrong side of the appliqué fabric shape. Dip the pounce or cotton swab in the starch and "paint" the starch over the seam allowance of the shape. Do not paint the edge that will lie under another piece, because that edge will not need to be basted. Wait a few minutes for the starch to penetrate the fabric. You can paint another shape and then go back to the first shape.

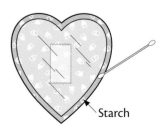

Starch

4. Using the template as a guide and with a dry iron, press the seam allowance over the edge of the plastic. Clip the seam allowances on inside curves and inside points to within one or two threads from the template, as needed. On outside curves, once you've achieved a smooth edge, flatten the seam allowance into little pleats, or clip the seam allowance so the fabric overlaps.

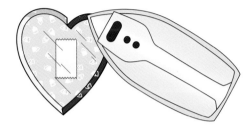

Pressing Tip

To keep from burning your fingers, use the pointed end of a 4" or 6" bamboo skewer or a wooden orange stick to manipulate the fabric around points and curves, and to hold the seam allowance in place while ironing.

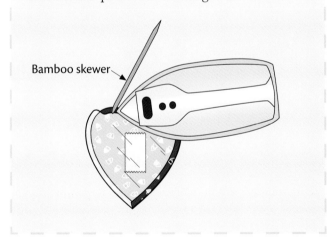

Bamboo skewer

5. For leaves and other pieces with outside points, fold one edge of the fabric over the template, extending the fold beyond the point of the template. Fold the other side in the same way. If you have a little fabric "flag" sticking out, fold the flag behind the point and press with your iron. There will probably be enough starch to hold the flag in place. If not, apply a small amount of starch and press again.

6. Allow the piece to cool; then remove the template and re-press if needed. Use one of the methods described below to stitch the appliqué pieces to the block background.

Hand Appliqué

1. Prepare the appliqué pieces as instructed in "Starch Appliqué" on page 8.

2. Follow the appliqué pattern or placement guide to position piece A on the background fabric. Pin or baste the piece in place.

3. Thread an appliqué needle with a thread color that matches the appliqué fabric. Use a traditional appliqué stitch to sew the piece to the background.

4. When the appliqué piece is completely stitched, remove the basting stitches. If you'll be hand quilting, you may want to cut away the excess background fabric behind the appliqué shape, leaving a ¼" seam allowance.

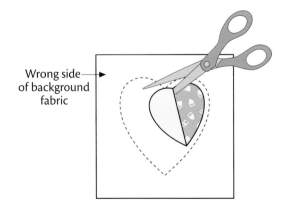

Wrong side of background fabric

5. Repeat steps 2–4 to position and appliqué the remaining pieces in alphabetical order. When all the appliqué is complete, gently press and square up the block, referring to "Squaring Up Blocks" on page 41.

Invisible Machine Appliqué

For this method, I like to use a very small machine blanket stitch, or you can use the blind hem stitch on your machine. You'll need to adjust the length and width of the stitches to use this method effectively. When done well, it's difficult to tell the results from hand appliqué.

1. Prepare the appliqué pieces as instructed in "Starch Appliqué" on page 8.

2. Thread the top of your machine with invisible thread (size .004). Thread the bobbin with a fine thread (60 weight) that matches the background fabric or, depending on your machine, you may want to try using invisible thread in your bobbin. When threading the bobbin with regular thread, bring the thread through the "finger" (if your machine has one) on the bobbin to slightly increase the bobbin tension. Reduce the top tension. Use a fine needle, size 60/8.

3. Use an open-toe embroidery presser foot and set the machine to the blanket stitch or blind hem stitch. Shorten the stitch length so that the distance the machine sews straight (between the stitches that swing to the left) is about ⅛". Adjust the stitch width so that the needle swings to the left no more than ¹⁄₁₆".

4. Make a test piece with fabrics scraps to check your stitch. Sew along the edge of a piece of folded fabric so that the straight stitches are in the background fabric, very close to the folded edge, and the swing stitch just catches the edge of the folded piece. The bobbin thread should not show on the top. Readjust the top tension as necessary to achieve the proper stitch.

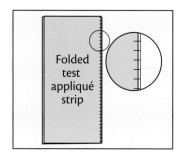

Folded test appliqué strip

5. Pin or use a little fabric glue to hold the piece in place on the block background. Position and appliqué the pieces in alphabetical order. Sew slowly,

turning and pivoting the block as needed. Make sure that any points are secured by a swing stitch on each side. Secure the thread ends by backstitching a few stitches. (The backstitches will not show on the front because of the invisible thread.)

Fabric Glue

There are a variety of fabric-basting glues and glue sticks available. Whatever you choose, make sure it will wash out after the project is done.

Fusible Appliqué

Fusible appliqué is extra fast and easy. With this technique, there are no seam allowances to turn under. I like to use a decorative stitch such as a machine blanket stitch or a zigzag stitch to secure the edges of the appliqué pieces. The decorative stitch adds texture, depth, and color to the project. You can use thread that matches the appliqué pieces or a contrasting thread. I use a 60-weight, 100%-cotton thread. I also use an open-toe embroidery foot so I can see the stitching line clearly.

Fusible web is available with smooth paper on one side and an adhesive on the reverse, or with paper on both sides and adhesive in the middle. There are many brands on the market, but I prefer Lite Steam-A-Seam 2, which has paper on both sides. When you purchase a fusible-web product, take time to read the manufacturer's instructions. Different products call for different heat settings and handling instructions. Be careful to not allow your hot iron to directly touch fusible web that is not covered by paper or fabric. I recommend using an appliqué pressing sheet or parchment paper.

1. Make a plastic template for each appliqué shape as described in "Making Appliqué Templates" on page 7. Place each template on the paper side of the fusible web, right side up, and trace around it. Use a pencil or permanent marker to trace each shape the number of times indicated on the pattern, leaving about ½" between shapes.

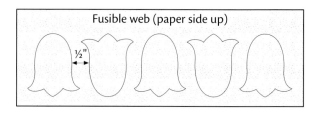

Fusible web (paper side up)

½"

2. Roughly cut the shape out of the fusible web, leaving about a ¼" margin all around the marked line. For larger pieces, or where pieces will be layered, cut out the center of the fusible-web shapes. Leave at least ¼" inside the line. This trimming allows the shape to adhere to the background and eliminates stiffness within the shape.

3. Place the shape, fusible-web side down, on the wrong side of the appropriate appliqué fabric. Following the manufacturer's instructions, iron in place. Let cool before handling.

4. Cut out the fabric shape on the drawn line and remove the paper backing.

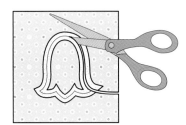

Removing the Paper

If you haven't cut away the center of the fusible web, try this tip. After cutting out the fabric shape on the drawn line, use a pin to score the paper in the center of the shape. Fold the shape along the scored line to loosen the paper, and then remove it from the fabric shape.

5. Using your pattern as a guide, position the appliqué shapes, adhesive side down, on the right side of the background fabric in alphabetical order and press.

6. When all of the pieces are fused, finish the edges with a decorative stitch, such as a machine blanket stitch. Sew so that the straight stitches are in the background fabric, very close to the appliqué edge, and the swing stitches are in the appliqué piece. Or instead of a blanket stitch, you could use a narrow zigzag stitch on the edges of the appliqué.

Blanket stitch   Zigzag stitch

EMBELLISHMENT

Some of the appliqué patterns include embellishments, which, of course, are optional or can be added using different methods. The line details can be drawn with a permanent pen. I like the Pigma Micro pen because it makes a fine line that doesn't bleed into the background. To draw a line, use the appliqué pattern and a light box or other light source. Start by tracing the line lightly, and then go back over the line several times until you've achieved the desired look.

To machine stitch or hand embroider the block details, use the appliqué pattern and a light box (or other light source), and lightly trace the line. If I'm using black thread, I use a permanent marker or fine-point mechanical pencil; however, if I'm using a thread color that matches the appliqué pieces, I use

a water-soluble marker. Before pressing, just be sure to remove the lines with water so they disappear. To machine stitch the line detail, use a short straight stitch and 30-weight thread. To hand embroider details, follow the instructions below to make a stem stitch.

Stem Stitch

Bring the needle up at A and down at B. Repeat, bringing the need up at C and down at D. Continue, keeping the thread on the same side of the stitching line.

BORDERS

Many quilts made in the 1930s are borderless because they were made from scraps, and yardage was scarce. If a quilt did have a border, the border was often cream or muslin. Today, most quilts have a border or borders that frame the pieced blocks. Borders can be simple strips of one or more fabrics. They can also be pieced or appliquéd and used in combination with plain strips. For the quilts in this book I've included a variety of borders. Of course, you may choose to omit a pieced border, but it will require yardage adjustments that have not been provided. On the other hand, I feel that making a pieced border is worth the extra effort.

Prepare border strips a few inches longer than you will actually need; then trim them to the correct length once you know the dimensions through the center of your quilt top. To find the correct measurement for the border strips, always measure through the center of the quilt, not along the outside edges. This ensures that the borders are of equal length on opposite sides of the quilt and helps keep your quilt square.

The border strips are generally cut crosswise, selvage to selvage, and joined end to end with a diagonal seam to achieve the desired length. Press the seam allowances open so they lie flat and are less conspicuous. Try to place the seams randomly around the quilt to make them even less noticeable.

Follow these instructions when adding borders with blunted corners to your quilt.

1. Lay two strips across the center of the quilt top from top to bottom. Trim both ends even with the raw edge of the quilt.

2. Mark the center of the border strips and the center of the sides of the quilt top. Pin the borders to the sides of the quilt top, matching centers and ends. Ease or slightly stretch the quilt top to fit the border strip as necessary. Sew the side borders in place with a ¼"-wide seam allowance and press the seam allowances toward the border strips.

Mark centers.

3. Repeat the process for the top and bottom borders, measuring through the borders you just added.

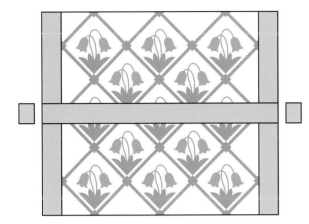

Pieced Borders

I love adding pieced borders—they can add a lot of interest to your quilt. However, they also require an accurate ¼" seam allowance and careful pressing so that everything will fit together correctly. You'll notice in the instructions that when a plain border is sewn to the quilt center prior to adding a pieced border, the plain border needs to be cut a specific length. It's important that the length of the plain border be accurate so that the pieced border will fit properly. Cut your plain borders to the specified length and ease them on the quilt if necessary. I've indicated the correct measurement of the quilt center, including the plain border and seam allowances, so that you can make sure your quilt is *mathematically* the correct size.

BINDING

I like a relatively narrow binding, often in a contrasting fabric. I prefer a double-fold binding made with strips cut 2" wide and sewn with a ¼" seam allowance. With the lightweight cotton battings I prefer, this strip-width and seam-allowance combination is perfect for completely filling the binding with batting, while still allowing the folded edge of the binding to just cover the stitching.

Beginner's Luck

Finished Quilt Size: 56½" x 56½"

Finished Block Size: 9"

Pieced and appliquéd by Nancy Mahoney; machine quilted by Nan Moore

The charming block in this quilt was one of the patterns from Laura Wheeler Designs. The block was originally designed for patchwork piecing with curved seams and several templates. I updated the construction for rotary cutting, and then used a starch appliqué technique to appliqué the quarter circles, making this block much easier to make. I had some triangle squares left over from another project and knew they'd make a wonderful sawtooth border. This is a superb project for using scraps or charm squares, so grab your scrap bag—you're sure to have fun making this delightful quilt!

Dateline–1931

* First nonstop flight across the Pacific Ocean completed in 41 hours, 13 minutes

* President Hoover signs an act making "The Star Spangled Banner" the national anthem

* The Empire State Building, the world's tallest structure, is dedicated in New York City

* Pearl S. Buck's book *The Good Earth* is released

* Academy Award winner for Best Picture of 1931 is *Cimarron*

MATERIALS

Yardages are based on 42"-wide fabrics.
Fat eighths measure 9" x 21".

150 squares, 5" x 5", **or** 3 yards *total* of assorted 1930s reproduction prints for blocks

2¾ yards of cream solid fabric for block background and borders

12 fat eighths of assorted blue 1930s reproduction prints for sawtooth border

½ yard of binding fabric

3¾ yards of backing fabric

62" x 62" piece of batting

Heat-resistant template plastic

CUTTING

Template pattern for the quarter circle appears on page 19. For detailed instructions, refer to "Making Appliqué Templates" on page 7.

From the cream solid fabric, cut:

2 strips, 5¾" x 42"; crosscut into 12 squares, 5¾" x 5¾"

7 strips, 4¾" x 42"; crosscut into:

> 100 rectangles, 2⅜" x 4¾"

> 4 squares, 2½" x 2½"

4 strips, 3½" x 42"; crosscut into 100 rectangles, 1½" x 3½"

6 outer-border strips, 2½" x 42"

5 inner-border strips, 2" x 42"

From the assorted 1930s reproduction prints, cut a total of:

50 squares, 3¾" x 3¾"; cut in half diagonally to yield 100 triangles

25 squares, 1½" x 1½"

100 quarter circles

From *each* of the 12 blue fat eighths, cut:

1 square, 5¾" x 5¾" (12 total)

From the binding fabric, cut:

6 strips, 2" x 42"

MAKING THE BLOCKS

Instructions are for making one block. Repeat to make a total of 25 blocks. After sewing each seam, press the seam allowances in the direction indicated by the arrows.

1. Sew two print triangles and one 1½" x 3½" cream rectangle together as shown. Make two.

Make 2.

2. Sew one print square between two 1½" x 3½" cream rectangles as shown.

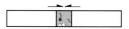

3. Sew the units from steps 1 and 2 together as shown.

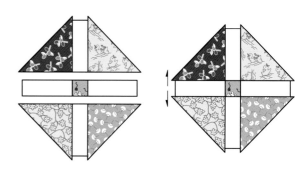

4. Position a 6½" square ruler on top of the unit, aligning the vertical and horizontal 3" lines on the ruler with the points on the center square, as shown. Trim two sides of the block. Turn the unit, realign the ruler, and trim the remaining sides. Each unit should measure 6" square.

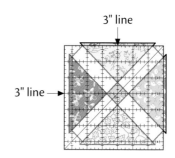

3" line

3" line →

5. Sew 2⅜" x 4¾" cream rectangles to opposite sides of the center unit from step 4 as shown. Sew cream rectangles to the two remaining sides.

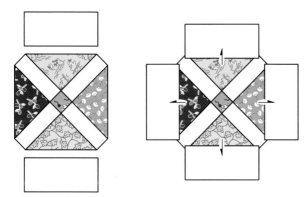

6. Referring to "Starch Appliqué" on page 8, prepare and appliqué four quarter circles to the unit from step 5 as shown to complete the block. Trim the seam allowances behind the appliquéd quarter circles, leaving a ¼" seam allowance. Make a total of 25 blocks.

Make 25.

ASSEMBLING THE QUILT TOP

1. Lay out five rows of five blocks each as shown in the quilt layout diagram on page 18. Sew the blocks together in rows, pressing the seam allowances in opposite directions from one row to the next. Sew the rows together and press the seam allowances in one direction.

2. Sew the 2"-wide cream inner-border strips together end to end. From this strip, cut two 45½"-long strips and sew them to opposite sides of the quilt top. Then cut two 48½"-long strips and sew them to the top and bottom of the quilt top. Press the seam allowances toward the just-added borders. The quilt top should measure 48½" square for the sawtooth border to fit properly.

Quick and Easy Triangle Squares

Over the years, I've seen various techniques for making triangle squares (also called half-square triangles) and have tried most of them with mixed results. Some of the techniques were a great addition to my bag of tricks, while others didn't give me the results I expected. When you need to make a lot of triangle squares—but still want a scrappy look—try using this method. To make triangle squares that measure 2" (finished size), you'll start with two 5¾" squares.

1. Draw intersecting diagonal lines from corner to corner on the wrong side of a 5¾" cream square. Layer the marked square with a 5¾" print square, right sides together and raw edges aligned. Stitch a scant ¼" on each side of both drawn diagonal lines.

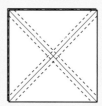

2. Carefully cut the squares apart horizontally and vertically as shown to yield four 2⅞" squares. Then cut the squares apart on the drawn diagonal line to yield eight triangle squares, each measuring 2½" square.

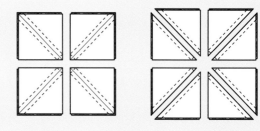

3. Referring to "Quick and Easy Triangle Squares" on page 17 and using the 5¾" cream squares and assorted blue squares, make 96 triangle squares. Press the seam allowances toward the blue triangles.

Make 96.

4. Lay out 24 triangle squares, making sure to arrange the blue triangles as shown. Sew the triangle squares together to make a sawtooth border strip. Make four border strips.

Make 4.

5. Sew sawtooth border strips to opposite sides of the quilt top. Press the seam allowances toward the inner-border strips. Sew 2½" cream squares to both ends of the two remaining border strips and press the seam allowances toward the cream squares. Sew these strips to the top and bottom of the quilt top.

6. Sew the 2½"-wide cream outer-border strips together end to end. Referring to "Borders" on page 12, measure the length of the quilt top; it should be 52½". Trim two cream strips to this length and sew them to the sides of the quilt top. Press the seam allowances toward the cream border. Measure the width of the quilt top; it should be 56½". Trim two cream strips to this length and sew them to the top and bottom of the quilt in the same manner.

Quilt layout

FINISHING

Cut and piece the backing fabric, and then layer the quilt top with batting and backing. After basting the layers together, hand or machine quilt as desired; see the quilting suggestion at right. Trim the batting and backing so the edges are even with the quilt top. Using the 2"-wide binding strips, make and attach binding.

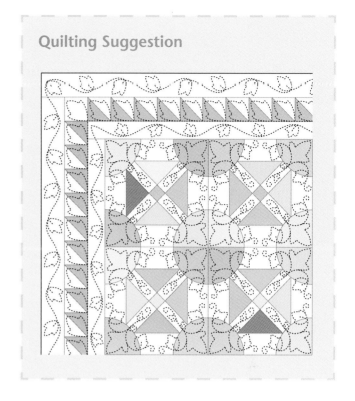

Quilting Suggestion

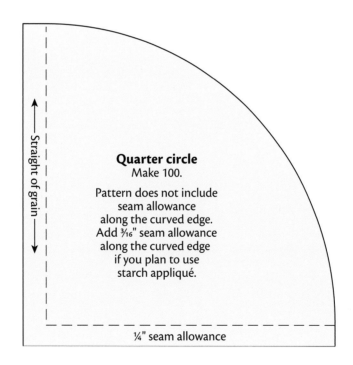

Quarter circle
Make 100.

Pattern does not include seam allowance along the curved edge. Add ³⁄₁₆" seam allowance along the curved edge if you plan to use starch appliqué.

Straight of grain

¼" seam allowance

Rose and Trellis

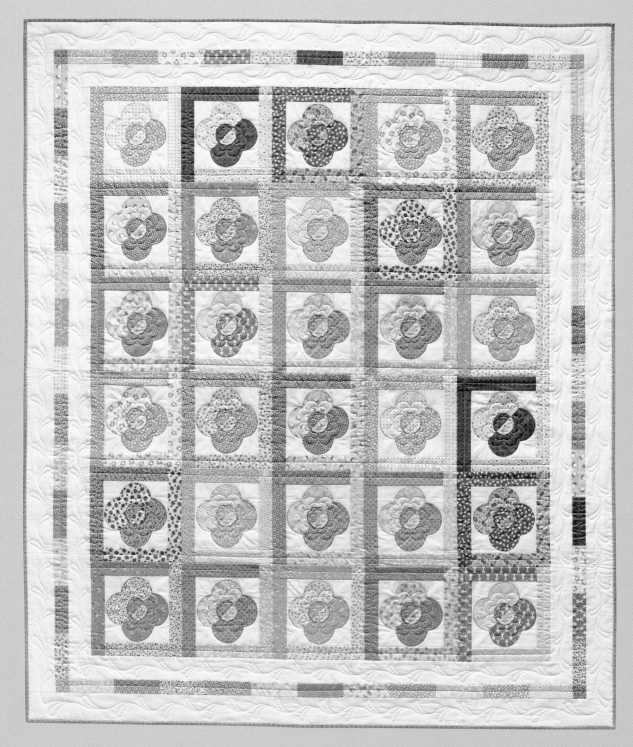

Finished Quilt Size: 64½" x 74½"

Finished Block Size: 10"

Pieced and appliquéd by Nancy Mahoney; machine quilted by Kelly Wise

This lovely Laura Wheeler design could be obtained from the *Clinton Herald* Needlecraft Department. Although the block was originally a patchwork design, I wouldn't dream of piecing the curved seams. Instead, I eliminated a few seam lines and converted the block to appliqué. Even though each block uses just two contrasting fabrics, I achieved a scrappy look by using a variety of prints. Then, using the rectangles as inspiration, I added an easy scrappy border to complete the design. This project is perfect for fusible appliqué, but be sure to use a lightweight fusible web so the appliqué isn't stiff.

Dateline–1932

* Amelia Earhart becomes the first woman to make a solo air crossing of the Atlantic Ocean

* Radio City Music Hall opens in New York City

* *Tarzan the Ape Man* opens, with Olympic gold-medal swimmer Johnny Weissmuller in the title role

* Books released include *Death in the Afternoon* by Ernest Hemingway and *The Thin Man* by Dashiell Hammett

* Academy Awards go to *Grand Hotel,* starring Greta Garbo and John Barrymore, for Best Picture of 1932 and to Walt Disney for inventing the character Mickey Mouse

MATERIALS

Yardages are based on 42"-wide fabrics.
Fat quarters measure 18" x 21".

15 fat quarters of assorted medium or dark 1930s reproduction prints for blocks and border

15 fat quarters of assorted light 1930s reproduction prints for blocks and border

3½ yards of cream solid fabric for block backgrounds and borders

⅝ yard of binding fabric

4 yards of backing fabric

70" x 80" piece of batting

3 yards of 16"-wide lightweight fusible web

Black or charcoal gray thread for appliqué

CUTTING

From the cream solid fabric, cut:

8 strips, 8½" x 42"; crosscut into 30 squares, 8½" x 8½". Cut each square in half diagonally to yield 60 triangles.

8 outer-border strips, 3½" x 42"

6 inner-border strips, 3" x 42"

From *each* of the assorted medium or dark 1930s reproduction prints, cut:

4 rectangles, 2" x 9" (60 total)

From the remaining assorted medium or dark 1930s reproduction prints, cut *a total of:*

22 rectangles, 2" x 5½"

4 squares, 2" x 2"

From *each* of the assorted light 1930s reproduction prints, cut:

4 rectangles, 2" x 9" (60 total)

From the remaining assorted light 1930s reproduction prints, cut *a total of:*

26 rectangles, 2" x 5½"

From the binding fabric, cut:

8 strips, 2" x 42"

MAKING THE BLOCKS

1. Referring to "Fusible Appliqué" on page 10 and using the patterns on page 25, prepare 15 light flower shapes and 15 medium or dark flower shapes with fusible web. Cut out the flower shapes on the drawn lines, and then cut the shapes in half on the center line. Lastly, carefully cut out the center half circle on the drawn line. Keep matching half-flower and half-circle pieces together.

2. Fold two cream triangles in half and finger-press to mark the center on the long side. Pair a light half flower and half circle with a medium/dark half flower and half circle; remove the paper backing and fuse a light half flower and medium/dark half circle to a cream triangle as shown. Fuse a medium/dark half flower and light half circle to a cream triangle. The pieces should not overlap; just position them so that the cut edges are abutted.

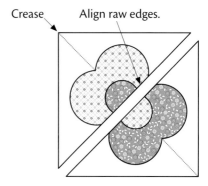

Crease   Align raw edges.

3. Machine blanket stitch along the curved edges using black or charcoal-gray thread. Be sure to stitch around both halves of the half circle and both halves of the flower or use a decorative stitch, such as a machine feather stitch to sew both sides at the same time.

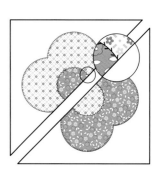

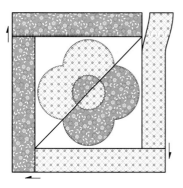

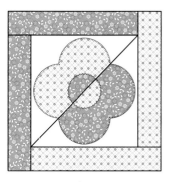

4. Pair a matching light flower triangle with a medium/dark flower triangle, and sew them together along their long edges as shown. Press the seam allowances open. Trim and square up the block center to 7½" x 7½".

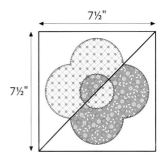

5. The rectangles surrounding the block center are stitched using a partial-seam technique. Lay out two 2" x 9" light rectangles and two 2" x 9" medium/dark rectangles that match the fabrics in the appliquéd center as shown. Sew a rectangle to the block center, stopping about 1" from the raw edge. Press the seam allowances toward the rectangle.

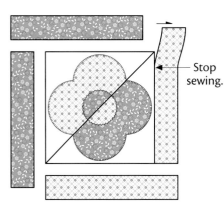

Stop sewing.

6. Working in a clockwise direction, sew a rectangle to the bottom, and then the left side of the appliquéd center. Sew the final rectangle to the appliquéd center. Press the seam allowances toward the just-added rectangles. Sew the open section closed

to complete the block. Repeat steps 2–6 to make a total of 30 blocks.

Make 30.

ASSEMBLING THE QUILT TOP

1. Lay out six rows of five blocks each as shown in the quilt layout diagram on page 24. Sew the blocks together in rows, pressing the seam allowances in opposite directions from one row to the next. Sew the rows together and press the seam allowances in one direction.

2. Sew the 3"-wide cream inner-border strips together end to end. From this strip, cut two 60½"-long strips and sew them to opposite sides of the quilt top. Then cut two 55½" long strips and sew them to the top and bottom of the quilt top. Press the seam allowances toward the just-added borders. The quilt top should measure 55½" x 65½" for the pieced border to fit properly.

3. To make the side pieced borders; lay out seven 2" x 5½" light rectangles and six 2" x 5½" dark rectangles, alternating them as shown. The border strip should start and end with a light rectangle. Sew the rectangles together; press the seam allowances open. Make two and sew them to the sides of the quilt top, pressing the seam allowances toward the cream inner border.

Make 2.

4. For the top pieced border, lay out six 2" x 5½" light rectangles and five 2" x 5½" dark rectangles, alternating them as shown. Sew the rectangles together; press the seam allowances open. Repeat to make a bottom border strip. Sew 2" squares to both ends of the strips as shown. Sew these borders to the quilt top and press the seam allowances toward the cream inner border.

Make 2.

5. Sew the 3½"-wide cream outer-border strips together end to end. Referring to "Borders" on page 12, measure the length of the quilt top; it should be 68½". Trim two cream strips to this length and sew them to the sides of the quilt top. Press the seam allowances toward the cream border. Measure the width of the quilt top; it should be 64½". Trim two cream strips to this length and sew them to the top and bottom of the quilt in the same manner.

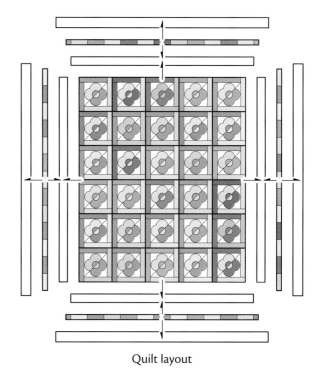

Quilt layout

FINISHING

Cut and piece the backing fabric, and then layer the quilt top with batting and backing. After basting the layers together, hand or machine quilt as desired; see the quilting suggestion below. Trim the batting and backing so the edges are even with the quilt top. Using the 2"-wide binding strips, make and attach binding.

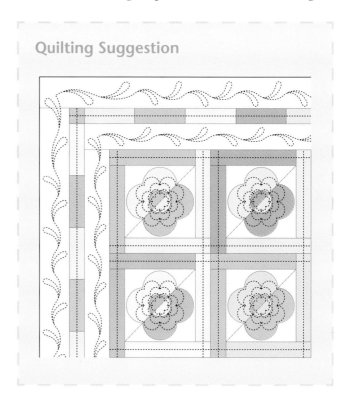

Quilting Suggestion

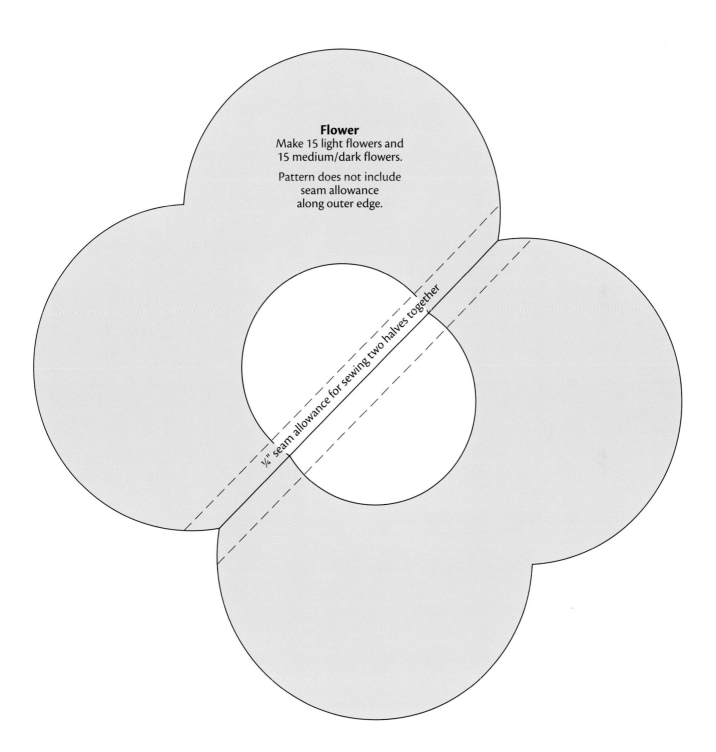

Flower
Make 15 light flowers and
15 medium/dark flowers.

Pattern does not include
seam allowance
along outer edge.

¼" seam allowance for sewing two halves together

Airship Propeller

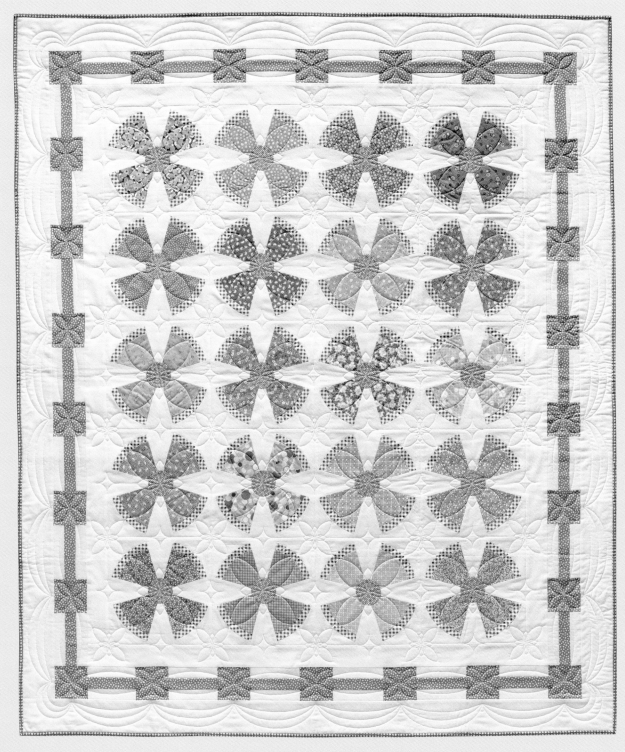

Finished Quilt Size: 54½" x 63½"

Finished Block Size: 9½"

Pieced and appliquéd by Nancy Mahoney; machine quilted by Kelly Wise

In 1933 *The Kansas City Star* described this block as follows: "Just as the steamboat and rail fence were inspirations to the colonial quiltmaker, the airplane is one to the modern woman. This propeller of the airship will mark the quilt of the vintage of 1900s." Air travel was in its infancy in the 1930s; no wonder quilters of the day were inspired by airplanes. Although the gentle curves in this block were originally pieced, I found it easier to appliqué them using the starch appliqué method. Each block uses a different print, but for continuity I used one green print for the centers, a green checked print for the outer edge of the blade, and a third green print for the pieced border.

Dateline–1933

* Worst year of the Great Depression

* Herbert Hoover is President until March 4; Franklin D. Roosevelt serves as President from March 4, 1933 to April 12, 1945

* Chicago World's Fair, A Century of Progress, opens

* Charles Darrow, an unemployed heating engineer, invents the game of MONOPOLY

* Fay Wray costars with a giant mechanical ape in *King Kong*

* Wiley Post completes a solo flight around the world in 7 days, 18 hours, 49 minutes

* Books released include *A Green Bough* by William Faulkner and *The Shape Of Things To Come* by H. G. Wells

* President Roosevelt created the Public Works of Art Project—the first federal government program to support the arts nationally

* Academy Award winner for Best Picture of 1933 is *Cavalcade*

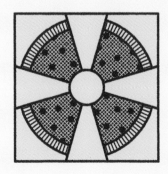

MATERIALS

Yardages are based on 42"-wide fabrics.
Fat eighths measure 9" x 21".

3 yards of cream solid fabric for blocks and borders

20 fat eighths **or** 1 yard *total* of assorted purple 1930s reproduction prints for blocks

¾ yard of dark green print for border

½ yard of green checked fabric for blocks

¼ yard of green dotted fabric for blocks

½ yard of binding fabric

3½ yards of backing fabric

60" x 69" piece of batting

Heat-resistant template plastic

CUTTING

Template patterns for pieces A–F appear on page 31. For detailed instructions, refer to "Making Appliqué Templates" on page 7.

From the cream solid fabric, cut:
6 outer-border strips, 3½" x 42"
5 inner-border strips, 2½" x 42"
8 strips, 1½" x 42"
80 of A
80 of D

From the green checked fabric, cut:
80 of B

From *each* of the 20 assorted purple prints, cut:
4 of C (80 total)

From the green dotted fabric, cut:
20 of E

From the dark green print, cut:
3 strips, 3½" x 42"; crosscut into 26 squares, 3½" x 3½"
4 strips, 1½" x 42"

From the binding fabric, cut:
7 strips, 2" x 42"

MAKING THE BLOCKS

Instructions are for making one block. Repeat to make a total of 20 blocks.

1. Referring to "Starch Appliqué" on page 8, prepare and appliqué the outside curve of a green checked B piece to a cream A piece as shown. Trim the seam allowances behind the appliquéd B pieces as needed, leaving a ¼" seam allowance. Make four.

Make 4.

2. Prepare and appliqué a purple C piece to each A/B unit as shown. Trim the seam allowances behind the appliquéd C pieces as needed, leaving a ¼" seam allowance. Make four matching units.

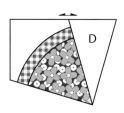

Make 4.

3. Sew a cream D piece to the right side of each unit from step 2 and press the seam allowances open. Make four matching units. Using a square ruler, trim any excess fabric along two sides as shown, making sure the center of each unit forms a 90° (right) angle. This little bit of trimming will help the blocks lie flat.

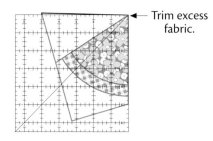

Make 4.

Trim excess fabric.

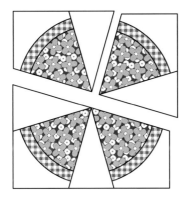

4. Arrange four units as shown. Sew the units together in pairs, and then sew the pairs together to complete the block. Press the seam allowances open. Don't worry about the center of the block; piece E will cover that potentially ugly spot.

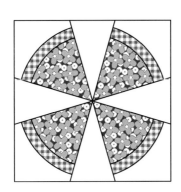

5. Hand baste a ring of gathering stitches about ⅛" from the outer edge of a green E circle. On the wrong side of the fabric circle, place the template in the center and pull the threads to gather the seam allowance over the edge of the template. Lightly dab the edge of the circle and the seam allowance with starch and press. Remove the template and gently pull the threads to tighten the circle again. Trim the threads. Appliqué the green circle in the center of the block. Make a total of 20 blocks, each measuring 10" square.

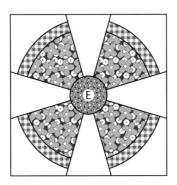

Make 20.

6. On the wrong side of each block, carefully remove a few stitches in a seam line behind the appliquéd circle. Then using sharp scissors, cut away the excess fabric behind the appliquéd circle, leaving at least ¼" seam allowance. Gently press the completed block.

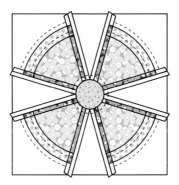

ASSEMBLING THE QUILT TOP

1. Lay out five rows of four blocks each as shown in the quilt layout diagram on page 30. Sew the blocks together in rows, pressing the seam allowances in opposite directions from one row to the next. Sew the rows together and press the seam allowances in one direction.

2. Sew the 2½"-wide cream inner-border strips together end to end. From this strip, cut two 48"-long strips and sew them to opposite sides of the quilt top. Then cut two 42½"-long strips and sew them to the top and bottom of the quilt top. Press the seam allowances toward the just-added borders. The quilt top should measure 42½" x 52" for the pieced border to fit properly.

3. For the pieced border, sew 1½"-wide cream strips to both long edges of a dark green strip as shown. Press the seam allowances toward the green strip. Make four strip sets. Crosscut the strip sets into the following segments:

    4 segments, 5⅜" wide

    10 segments, 5¼" wide

    12 segments, 5" wide

Make 4.

4. For the pieced side borders, sew together six 3½" dark green squares and five 5¼"-wide segments as shown to make a border strip. Sew a 5⅜"-wide segment to each end of the strip. The strip should be 52" long. Make two and sew them to the sides of the quilt top.

5⅜" 5¼"   5⅜"

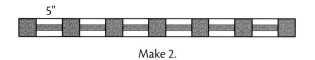

Make 2.

5. For the top and bottom borders, sew together seven 3½" dark green squares and six 5"-wide segments as shown to make a border strip. Make two and sew them to the quilt top.

5"

Make 2.

6. Sew the 3½"-wide cream outer-border strips together end to end. Referring to "Borders" on page 12, measure the length of the quilt top; it should be 58". Trim two cream strips to this length and sew them to the sides of the quilt top. Press the seam allowances toward the cream border. Measure the width of the quilt top; it should be 54½". Trim two cream strips to this length and sew them to the top and bottom of the quilt in the same manner.

FINISHING

Cut and piece the backing fabric, and then layer the quilt top with batting and backing. After basting the layers together, hand or machine quilt as desired; see the quilting suggestion below. Trim the batting and backing so the edges are even with the quilt top. Using the 2"-wide binding strips, make and attach binding.

Quilting Suggestion

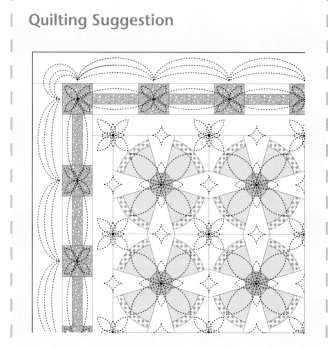

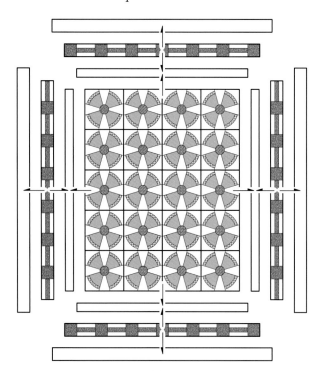

Quilt layout

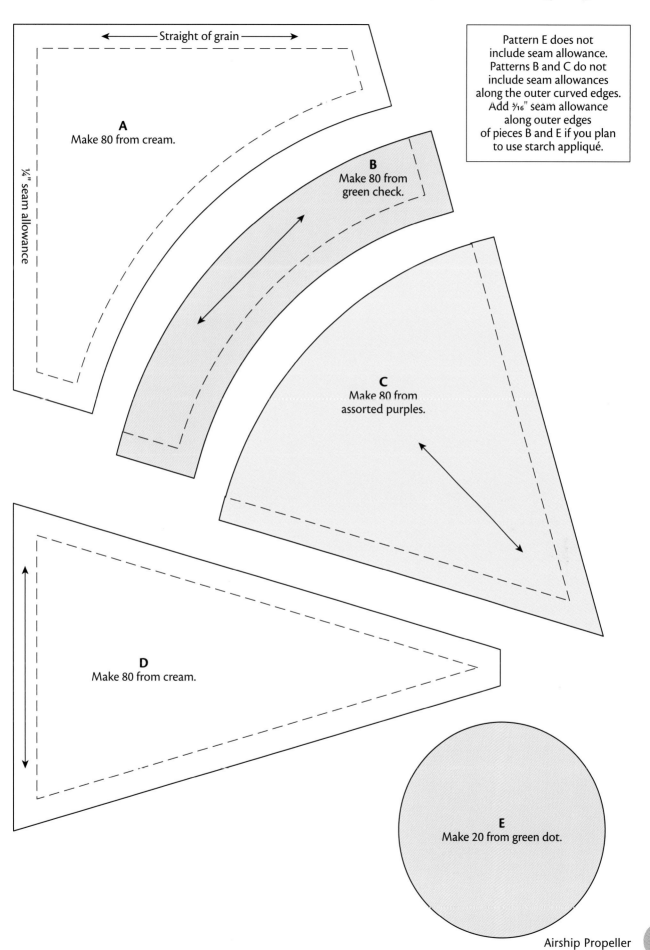

Pattern E does not
include seam allowance.
Patterns B and C do not
include seam allowances
along the outer curved edges.
Add ³⁄₁₆" seam allowance
along outer edges
of pieces B and E if you plan
to use starch appliqué.

Straight of grain

¼" seam allowance

A
Make 80 from cream.

B
Make 80 from
green check.

C
Make 80 from
assorted purples.

D
Make 80 from cream.

E
Make 20 from green dot.

Airship Propeller

Cowboy's Star

Finished Quilt Size: 53" x 53"

Finished Block Size: 9½"

Pieced and appliquéd by Nancy Mahoney; machine quilted by Kelly Wise

I admit I love star blocks, and when I found this one, I had to have it. This delightful but tricky block is from Laura Wheeler Designs and was available from the *Clinton Herald*. At first, I was going to piece all of those curves. But I soon realized I could straighten a couple lines and appliqué the remaining curves. Then, to avoid matching the corners of the blocks, I added narrow sashing so the blocks float just a little. The block is still a bit fiddly, but the only really tough part is matching the centers. You only have to make 16 blocks, and your friends will be so impressed!

Dateline–1934

* Stamps are 3¢

* Donald Duck appears for the first time in *The Wise Little Hen*

* First annual Masters Golf Tournament is held in Augusta, Georgia

* Books released include *Goodbye, Mr. Chips* by James Hilton and *Tender is the Night* by F. Scott Fitzgerald

* The film *Stand Up and Cheer* is released with five-year-old Shirley Temple in a relatively minor role; later in the year she goes on to sing "The Good Ship Lollipop" in the film *Bright Eyes*

* Academy Award winner for Best Picture of 1934 is *It Happened One Night*, starring Clark Gable

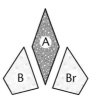

MATERIALS

Yardages are based on 42"-wide fabrics.

1⅞ yards of cream solid fabric for blocks, sashing, and border

1⅜ yards of red 1930s reproduction print for blocks and border

1⅛ yards of blue 1930s reproduction print for blocks, border, and binding

½ yard of yellow 1930s reproduction print for blocks

3⅜ yards of backing fabric

58" x 58" piece of batting

Heat-resistant template plastic

CUTTING

Template patterns for pieces A–E appear on page 37. For detailed instructions, refer to "Making Appliqué Templates" on page 7.

From the blue print, cut:

11 strips, 2" x 42" (5 for middle border, 6 for binding)

6 strips, 1⅞" x 42"; crosscut into 64 of A

From the yellow print, cut:

4 strips, 2¼" x 42"; crosscut into 64 of B *and* 64 of B reversed

From the red print, cut:

6 outer-border strips, 4½" x 42"

4 strips, 4" x 42"; crosscut into 64 of C

From the cream solid fabric, cut:

3 strips, 4½" x 42"; crosscut into 64 of D

16 strips, 2" x 42"; crosscut into 64 of E

5 inner-border strips, 1½" x 42"

6 strips, 1" x 42"; crosscut into:

    3 sashing strips, 1" x 40"

    12 sashing strips, 1" x 10"

MAKING THE BLOCKS

Instructions are for making one block. Repeat to make a total of 16 blocks. After sewing each seam, press the seam allowances in the direction indicated by the arrows.

1. Lay out one blue A piece, one yellow B piece, and one yellow B reversed piece as shown. With the ends of the pieces offset as shown, sew the pieces together. Make four.

Make 4.

2. Referring to "Starch Appliqué" on page 8, prepare and appliqué a red C piece to each unit from step 1 as shown. Trim the seam allowances behind the appliquéd red piece, leaving a ¼" seam allowance. Make four.

Make 4.

3. Sew a cream D piece to the right side of each unit from step 2, offsetting the ends as shown. Make four. Using a square ruler, trim any excess fabric along two sides as shown, making sure the center of each unit forms a 90° (right) angle. This little bit of trimming will make sewing the units together easier and help the block lie flat!

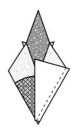
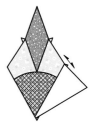

Make 4.

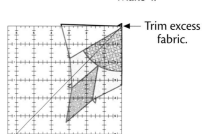

Trim excess fabric.

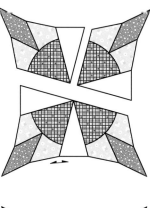

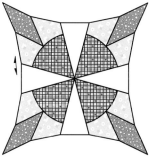

4. Arrange four units as shown. Sew the units together in pairs, and then sew the pairs together, matching the seam intersections.

5. Again, referring to "Starch Appliqué" as needed, prepare and appliqué four cream E pieces to the unit from step 4 as shown to complete the block. Trim the seam allowances behind the appliquéd E pieces, leaving a ¼" seam allowance. Make a total of 16 blocks, each measuring 10" square.

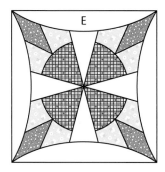

E

Make 16.

Placement Guide

You'll find it easier to position the E piece correctly if you use a placement guide. Draw a 10" square on a large piece of paper; then draw intersecting diagonal lines from corner to corner *and* horizontal and vertical lines to establish centering lines. Fold the star unit in half vertically and horizontally and finger-press to crease. Lay the placement guide on your ironing board and place the star unit on top of it. Align the star points with the diagonal lines and the creases with the horizontal and vertical lines. Pin the star unit in place by inserting pins through the unit into the ironing board pad. Next, fold the prepared E pieces in half and finger-press to mark the center on the curved edge. On two adjacent sides, align the straight edge of an E piece with the drawn square and match the center creases. The E pieces should overlap slightly in the corner and the point of the star unit should be ¼" from the outer edge. Glue baste in place. Add E pieces to the remaining two sides, making sure to align the straight edges. You should have a ¼" seam allowance beyond the star point in each corner.

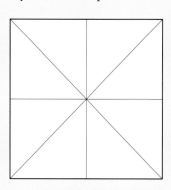

Draw centering lines.

¼"

¼"

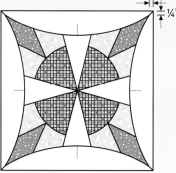

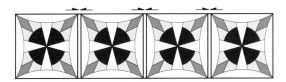

ASSEMBLING THE QUILT TOP

1. Lay out four blocks and three 1" x 10" cream sashing strips as shown. Sew the pieces together to make a block row, pressing the seam allowances toward the sashing strips. Make 4 block rows total. The block rows should be 40" long.

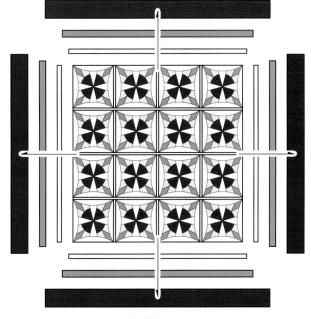

Make 4.

2. Lay out the four block rows and three 1" x 40" sashing strips as shown in the quilt layout diagram. Sew the rows and sashing strips together and press the seam allowances toward the sashing strips.

3. Sew the 1½"-wide cream inner-border strips together end to end. Referring to "Borders" on page 12, measure the length of the quilt top; trim two cream strips to this length and sew them to the sides of the quilt top. Measure the width of the quilt top; trim two cream strips to this length and sew them to the top and bottom of the quilt in the same manner. Press the seam allowances toward the just-added borders.

4. In the same manner, sew five 2"-wide blue middle-border strips together end to end, and then measure, cut, and sew the strips to the quilt top for the middle border, pressing as shown above right. Lastly, sew the 4½"-wide red outer-border strips end to end; measure, cut, and sew them to the quilt top for the outer border, pressing as shown.

Quilt layout

FINISHING

Cut and piece the backing fabric, and then layer the quilt top with batting and backing. After basting the layers together, hand or machine quilt as desired; see the quilting suggestion below. Trim the batting and backing so the edges are even with the quilt top. Using the remaining 2"-wide blue strips, make and attach binding.

Quilting Suggestion

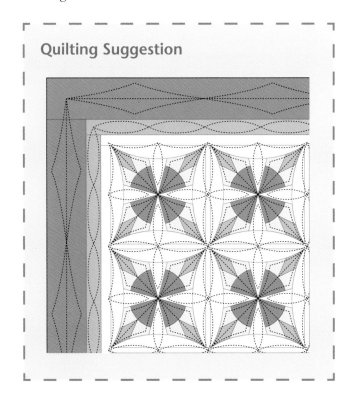

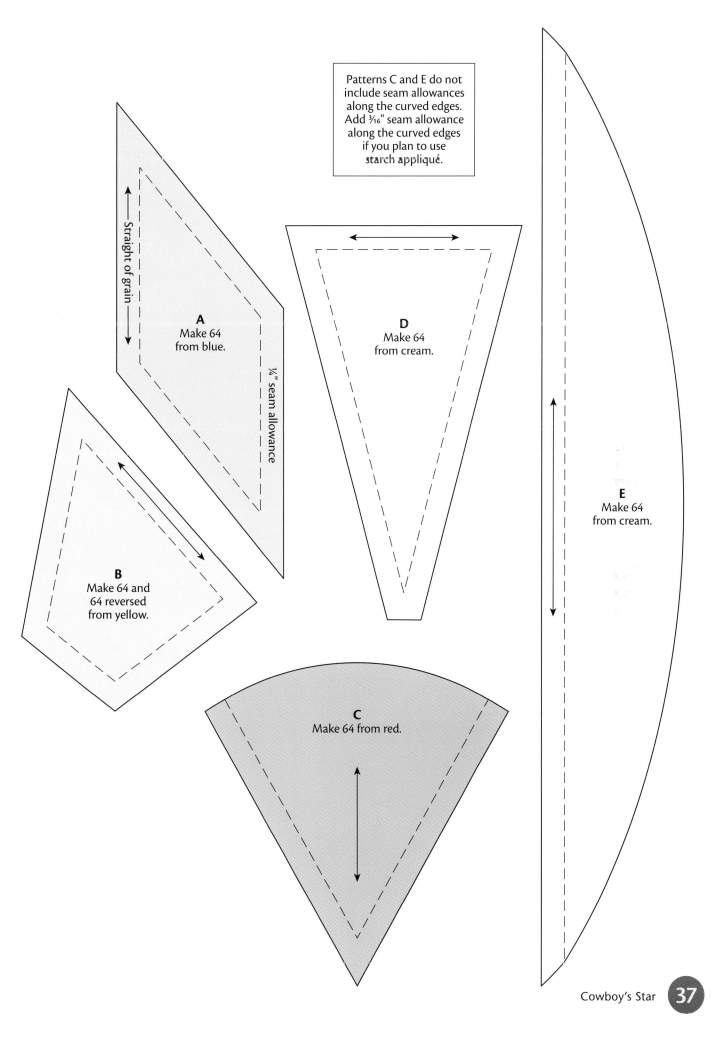

Patterns C and E do not
include seam allowances
along the curved edges.
Add ³⁄₁₆" seam allowance
along the curved edges
if you plan to use
starch appliqué.

Straight of grain

A
Make 64
from blue.

¼" seam allowance

B
Make 64 and
64 reversed
from yellow.

D
Make 64
from cream.

C
Make 64 from red.

E
Make 64
from cream.

Bell Flowers

Finished Quilt Size: 64" x 64"

Finished Block Size: 10"

Pieced and appliquéd by Nancy Mahoney; machine quilted by Nan Moore

This darling Laura Wheeler block was available from Needlecraft Service, Old Chelsea Station, in New York City. The postage on the original envelope is 2½ cents, dating it between 1931 and 1933. During the 1930s, realistic-looking flowers were a popular appliqué design. I particularly like the graceful stems and delicate flowers in this block. Surprisingly the block was unnamed, so I called it Bell Flowers. For each flower, I chose a different print in one color family, ranging from peach to red, and then used one green for the leaves and sashing to tie it all together. This delightful quilt will convey a touch of spring all year long.

Dateline–1935

* Amelia Earhart becomes the first person to fly solo between Honolulu, Hawaii, and Oakland, California

* Babe Ruth retires from professional baseball with 714 home runs

* Benny Goodman, "the King of Swing," opens at the Palomar Ballroom in Los Angeles

* George and Ira Gershwin's musical, *Porgy and Bess*, opens in New York

* The DC-3 (Douglas 1935) travels nonstop across the country in 15 hours

* Books released include *Of Time and the River* by Thomas Wolfe and *Tortilla Flat* by John Steinbeck

* Academy Award winner for Best Picture of 1935 is *Mutiny on the Bounty*

MATERIALS

Yardages are based on 42"-wide fabrics.
Fat quarters measure 18" x 21".

3 yards of cream solid fabric for blocks, sashing, and setting triangles

2 yards of green 1930s reproduction print for leaf and stem appliqués, sashing, and border

1¾ yards of pink floral 1930s reproduction print for border and binding

26 squares, 5" x 5", **or** ⅔ yards *total* of assorted pink, peach and red 1930s reproduction prints for flower appliqués

4 yards of backing fabric

69" x 69" piece of batting

2½ yards of 16"-wide lightweight fusible web (optional)

Pink, peach and red thread to match for appliqué

30-weight cotton or rayon thread (or 6-strand embroidery floss) to match for appliqué details

Template plastic

CUTTING

From the cream solid fabric, cut:

5 strips, 11" x 42"; crosscut into:

    13 squares, 11" x 11"

    2 squares, 8¼" x 8¼"; cut once diagonally to yield 4 corner triangles

24 strips, 1⅛" x 42"

2 squares, 15½" x 15½"; cut twice diagonally to yield 8 side triangles

From the green print, cut:

6 inner-border strips, 1¾" x 42"

12 strips, 1¼" x 42"

3 squares, 4½" x 4½"; cut twice diagonally to yield 12 quarter-square triangles

12 squares, 2½" x 2½"

From the *bias* of the remaining green print, cut:

13 strips, ½" x 14"

13 strips, ½" x 9"

From the pink floral print, cut:

7 outer-border strips, 5½" x 42"

7 binding strips, 2" x 42"

MAKING THE BLOCKS

1. To make the stems, place one end of a ½"-wide bias strip into a ¼" bias-tape maker. Pull just the tip of the strip through the bias-tape maker and pin it to your ironing board. Continue to pull the bias-tape maker slowly along the strip, following close behind it with your iron to crease the edges of the fabric as it emerges from the bias-tape maker. Make 13 short stems and 13 long stems.

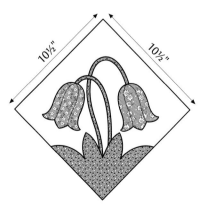

2. Choose your favorite appliqué method and make appliqué templates for the flower and leaf by tracing the patterns on pages 42 and 43. Refer to "Appliqué Techniques" on page 7 for details as needed. Make two flowers using the assorted pink, peach, or red squares, and one green leaf for each block. Refer to the photo on page 38 for color placement ideas.

3. Fold each 11" cream square in half vertically and horizontally and lightly finger-press to create centerlines. Using the photo and the appliqué placement guide on page 43 and starting with a long stem, position one long and one short stem on a cream square. Be sure the squares are positioned on point. Appliqué the stems in place. Then position and appliqué two flowers and one leaf in place. Leave the bottom of the leaf unstitched; it will be sewn into the seam line. To add the stitching line details, use a straight stitch on your sewing machine, or hand embroider a stem stitch.

4. Make 13 appliqué blocks. Gently press, and then trim each block to 10½" x 10½", referring to "Squaring Up Blocks" on page 41.

Make 13.

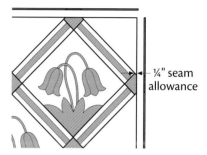

ASSEMBLING THE QUILT TOP

1. For the pieced sashing, sew 1⅛"-wide cream strips to both long edges of a 1¼"-wide green strip as shown. Make 12 strip sets. From the strip sets, cut 36 segments, 10½" wide.

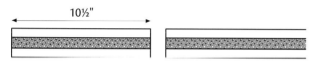

10½"

Make 12 strip sets.
Cut 36 segments.

2. Refer to the quilt layout diagram to arrange the blocks, pieced sashing strips, green squares, green quarter-square triangles, cream side triangles, and cream corner triangles in diagonal rows as shown.

3. Sew the pieces in each row together; press the seam allowances toward the sashing strips. Sew the rows together and add the corner triangles last; again press the seam allowances toward the sashing strips. Note that the green and cream triangles are a bit oversized and will be trimmed in the next step.

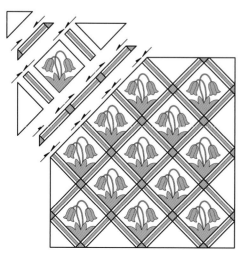

Quilt layout

4. To trim and straighten the quilt top, align the ¼" line on your ruler with the outermost points of the sashing strips. Use a rotary cutter to trim any excess fabric, leaving a ¼" seam allowance. Square the corners of the quilt top as necessary.

¼" seam allowance

5. Sew the 1¾"-wide green inner-border strips together end to end. Referring to "Borders" on page 12, measure the length of the quilt top. Trim two strips to this length and sew them to the sides of the quilt top for the inner border. Press the seam allowances toward the border. Measure the width of the quilt top; trim two strips to this length and sew them to the top and bottom of the quilt. Press the seam allowances toward the border.

6. For the outer border, sew three of the 5½"-wide pink floral strips end to end for the side borders. Measure the length of the quilt top; trim two strips to this length and sew them to the sides of the quilt top. Then sew the remaining 5½"-wide pink floral strips in pairs. Measure the width of the quilt top; trim two strips to this length and sew them to the top and bottom of the quilt top. Press the seam allowances toward the just-added borders.

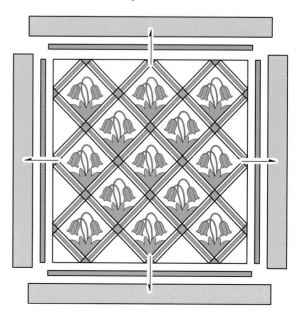

FINISHING

Cut and piece the backing fabric, and then layer the quilt top with batting and backing. After basting the layers together, hand or machine quilt as desired; see the quilting suggestion at right. Trim the batting and backing so the edges are even with the quilt top. Using the 2"-wide pink floral strips, make and attach binding.

Quilting Suggestion

Pattern does not include seam allowance along curved edges.

Align with edge of block.

Leaf
Make 13 from green.

¼" seam allowance

Align with edge of block.

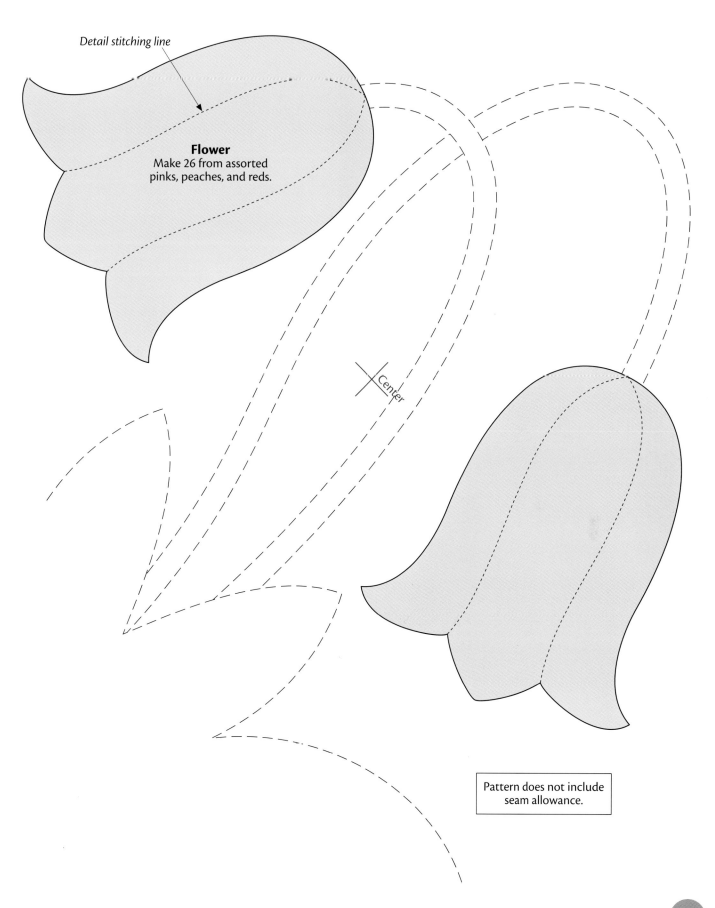

Detail stitching line

Flower
Make 26 from assorted
pinks, peaches, and reds.

Center

Pattern does not include
seam allowance.

Whirling Fans

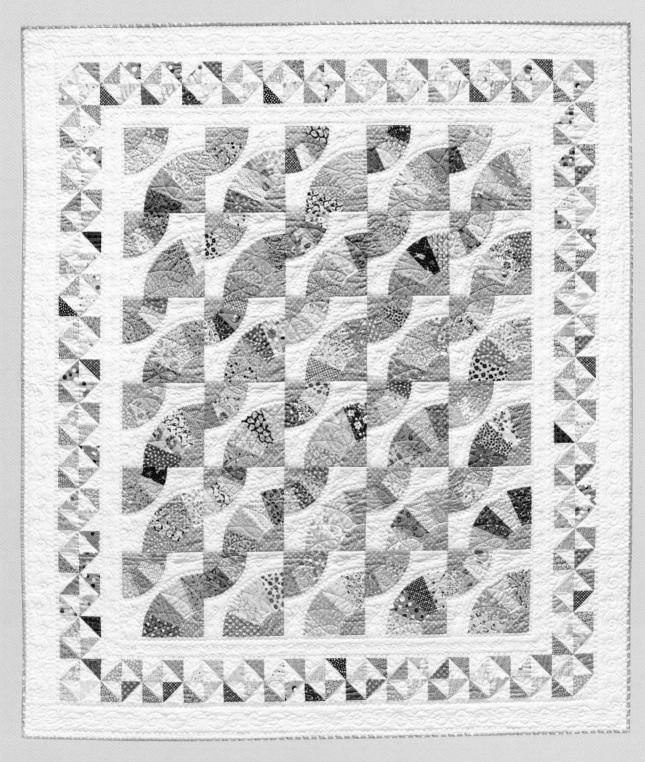

Finished Quilt Size: 59½" x 67½"

Finished Block Size: 8"

Pieced and appliquéd by Nancy Mahoney; machine quilted by Nan Moore

Fan blocks and fan quilts are another favorite design of mine. I have at least three vintage fan quilts and have made several quilts using different fan blocks. So when I came across this Double Fan block designed by Alice Brooks, I was smitten. This design is ideal for charm squares or for using up lots of little scraps. As I was rummaging through my scrap bags, I found some leftover print triangles already paired with cream triangles from another project. What a find! With the addition of a few more triangle squares, I knew they'd be perfect for the Broken Dishes blocks in the border. Don't you love happy endings?

Dateline–1936

* Margaret Mitchell publishes her only book *Gone with the Wind*

* Popular films include *Follow the Fleet*, starring Fred Astaire and Ginger Rogers; *Flash Gordon*; and *The Oregon Trail*

* The SS Queen Mary arrives in New York City on her maiden voyage from England

* San Francisco's Bay Bridge is completed linking San Francisco and Oakland

* Generators at Hoover Dam began transmitting electricity from the Colorado River 266 miles to Los Angeles, California

* Robert Frost's *A Further Range* wins a Pulitzer Prize

* Academy Award winner for Best Picture of 1936 is *The Great Ziegfeld*

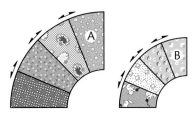

MATERIALS

Yardages are based on 42"-wide fabrics.

4¼ yards of cream solid fabric for blocks and borders

120 squares, 5" x 5", **or** 1⅞ yards *total* of assorted 1930s reproduction prints for Fan blocks

1 yard of green 1930s reproduction print for Fan blocks

26 squares, 6" x 6", **or** 1 yard *total* of assorted 1930s reproduction prints for Broken Dishes blocks

½ yard of binding fabric

3¾ yards of backing fabric

65" x 73" piece of batting

Template plastic

CUTTING

Template patterns for pieces A, B, C, and D appear on page 49. For detailed instructions, refer to "Making Appliqué Templates" on page 7.

From the cream solid fabric, cut:

8 strips, 8½" x 42"; crosscut into 30 squares, 8½" x 8½"

5 strips, 5¾" x 42"; crosscut into 26 squares, 5¾" x 5¾"

7 outer-border strips, 4" x 42"

5 inner-border strips, 2½" x 42"

From *each* of the 5" squares, cut:

1 of A (120 total)

1 of B (120 total)

From the green print, cut:

30 of C

30 of D

From *each* of the 6" squares, cut:

1 square, 5¾" x 5¾" (26 total)

From the binding fabric, cut:

7 strips, 2" x 42"

MAKING THE FAN BLOCKS

1. Sew together four A pieces as shown. Sew together four B pieces as shown. Press the seam allowances open to reduce bulk. Make 30 large fan units and 30 small fan units.

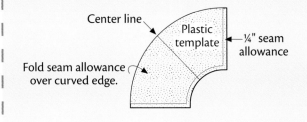

Make 30 of each.

2. Fold the seam allowance along the curved top edge of each fan unit to the wrong side and press in place to make a finished edge. It doesn't matter if the seam allowance is not a uniform width, but you do want a smooth finished curve.

Smooth Curves

An easy way to achieve a smooth curved edge on the fan units is to make a template using heat-resistant plastic. To do this, trace four large fan blades (A) side by side onto a piece of paper. You don't need the seam allowance between the blades or along the curved edge, but trace a ¼" seam allowance along the side edges and inside curve. Use the traced pattern to make a plastic template for the large fan unit. Mark the center seam line for placement guidance. Repeat to make a plastic template for the small fan unit. Referring to "Starch Appliqué" on page 8, place the plastic template on the wrong side of the fan unit and press the seam allowance over the edge of the template.

Center line
Plastic template
¼" seam allowance
Fold seam allowance over curved edge.

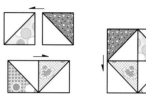

3. Fold an 8½" cream square in half diagonally and lightly finger-press to create a center line. Place a large fan unit in one corner, matching the center seam line with the creased line, and then place a small fan unit in the opposite corner. Referring to "Starch Appliqué" on page 8, prepare 30 green C pieces and 30 green D pieces. Place a C piece along the base of the large fan unit and a D along the base of the small fan unit. Appliqué the pieces in place along the curved edges. Note that the sides of the fans will be sewn into the block seam. Make 30 Double Fan blocks. Gently press and then trim each block to 8½" x 8½" as needed.

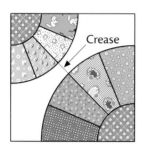

Crease

Make 30.

MAKING THE BROKEN DISHES BLOCKS

1. Referring to "Quick and Easy Triangle Squares" on page 17 and using the 5¾" cream squares and assorted print squares, make a total of 208 triangle squares. Press the seam allowances toward the print triangles.

2. Lay out four triangle squares in a four-patch arrangement as shown above right. Sew the squares together in rows, and then sew the rows together. To reduce bulk in the center of the block and create opposing seams, use a seam ripper to remove one

or two stitches from the seam allowance. Gently reposition the seam allowances to evenly distribute the fabric and press them in opposite directions. Make 52 Broken Dishes blocks.

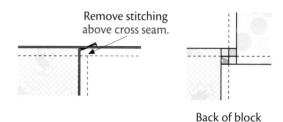

Make 52.

Remove stitching above cross seam.

Back of block

ASSEMBLING THE QUILT TOP

1. Lay out six rows of five blocks each as shown in the quilt layout diagram on page 48. Sew the blocks together in rows, pressing the seam allowances in opposite directions from one row to the next. Sew the rows together and press the seam allowances in one direction.

2. Sew the 2½"-wide cream inner-border strips together end to end. From this strip, cut two 48½"-long strips and sew them to opposite sides of the quilt top. Then cut two 44½"-long strips and sew them to the top and bottom of the quilt top. Press the seam allowances toward the just-added borders. The quilt top should measure 44½" x 52½" for the Broken Dishes border to fit properly.

3. Lay out 13 Broken Dishes blocks as shown. Sew the blocks together to make a side border. Repeat to make a second side border. Lay out 13 blocks as shown and sew them together to make the top border. Repeat to make the bottom border. Note that the blocks in the side borders are oriented differently than those in the top and bottom borders. Press the seam allowances as indicated by the arrows.

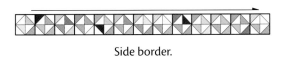

Side border.
Make 2.

Top/bottom border.
Make 2.

4. Sew the border strips from step 3 to the sides, and then the top and bottom of the quilt top. Press the seam allowances toward the cream inner-border.

5. Sew the 4"-wide cream outer-border strips together end to end. Referring to "Borders" on page 12, measure the length of the quilt top; it should be 60½". Trim two cream strips to this length and sew them to the sides of the quilt top. Press the seam allowances toward the cream border. Measure the width of the quilt top; it should be 59½". Trim two cream strips to this length and sew them to the top and bottom of the quilt in the same manner.

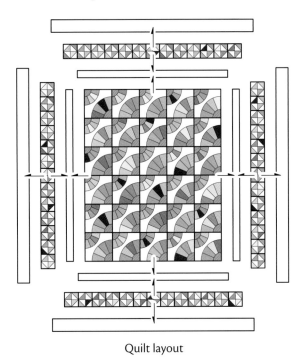

Quilt layout

FINISHING

Cut and piece the backing fabric, and then layer the quilt top with batting and backing. After basting the layers together, hand or machine quilt as desired; see the quilting suggestion below. Trim the batting and backing so the edges are even with the quilt top. Using the 2"-wide binding strips, make and attach the binding.

Quilting Suggestion

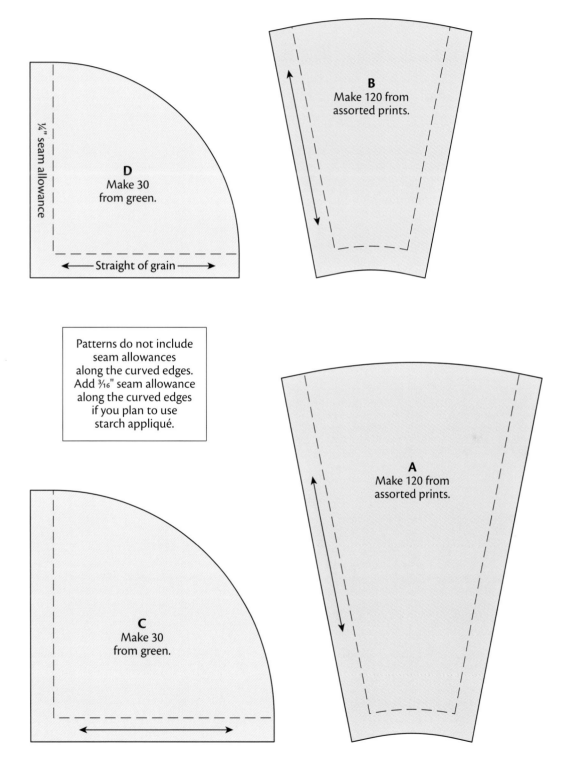

D
Make 30
from green.

¼" seam allowance

Straight of grain

B
Make 120 from
assorted prints.

Patterns do not include
seam allowances
along the curved edges.
Add ³⁄₁₆" seam allowance
along the curved edges
if you plan to use
starch appliqué.

A
Make 120 from
assorted prints.

C
Make 30
from green.

Coming Up Roses

Finished Quilt Size: 53¾" x 70"

Finished Block Size: 8"

Pieced and appliquéd by Nancy Mahoney; machine quilted by Kelly Wise

This Rose appliqué block was designed by Alice Brooks. As Gypsy Rose Lee once said, "everything's coming up roses," and in this delightfully scrappy quilt, it's all about the roses. In nature, no two roses are alike, so I made all of mine different—but used one green print for the leaves, which adds continuity to the design. Then I pieced the setting triangles so it appears that the blocks are spilling over a yellow border. Stop and smell the roses!

Dateline–1937

* Books released include *Death on the Nile* by Agatha Christie, *The Hobbit* by J. R. R. Tolkien, and *Of Mice and Men* by John Steinbeck

* The Golden Gate Bridge opens in San Francisco

* The first Blood Bank opens in Chicago

* Dupont patents nylon, invented by Wallace H. Carothers

* *Snow White and the Seven Dwarfs* premieres at the Carthay Circle Theatre on December 21, 1937. It's the first full-length animated feature in full color and sound, and the first of the Walt Disney Animated Classics.

* Academy Award winner for Best Picture of 1937 is *Life of Emile Zola*

MATERIALS

Yardages are based on 42"-wide fabrics.
Fat quarters measure 18" x 21".

2⅞ yards of cream solid fabric for blocks, setting triangles, and inner border

32 squares, 7" x 7", **or** 1½ yards *total* of assorted 1930s reproduction prints for rose appliqués

1⅛ yards of pink 1930s reproduction print for outer border and binding

⅞ yard of yellow 1930s reproduction print for setting triangles

⅞ yard of mint-green 1930s reproduction print for middle border

⅔ yard of green 1930s reproduction print for leaf appliqués

3¾ yard of backing fabric

63" x 75" piece of batting

3⅝ yards of 16"-wide lightweight fusible web (optional)

Pink, peach, red, lilac, and yellow thread to match for appliqué

30-weight cotton or rayon thread (or 6-strand embroidery floss) to match for appliqué details

Template plastic

CUTTING

From the cream solid fabric, cut:

8 strips, 9" x 42"; crosscut into 32 squares, 9" x 9"

2 strips, 4½" x 42"; crosscut into 14 squares, 4½" x 4½"

6 inner-border strips, 1¾" x 42"

From the yellow print, cut:

4 squares, 13" x 13"; cut twice diagonally to yield 16 quarter-square triangles (2 will be extra)

2 squares, 7" x 7"; cut once diagonally to yield 4 corner triangles

From the mint-green print, cut:

7 middle-border strips, 3½" x 42"

From the pink print, cut:

7 outer-border strips, 2½" x 42"

7 binding strips, 2" x 42"

MAKING THE BLOCKS

1. Choose your favorite appliqué method and make appliqué templates for the flower and leaves by tracing the patterns on page 55. Refer to "Appliqué Techniques" on page 7 for details as needed. For each block, make one flower using the assorted prints and two leaves using the green print. Refer to the photo on page 50 for color placement ideas.

2. Fold each 9" cream square in half diagonally in both directions and finger-press to establish centering lines. Using the photo and the appliqué pattern as a placement guide and starting with the leaves, position and appliqué two leaves and one flower in the center of a cream square. Be sure the squares are positioned on point. To add the stitching line details, use a straight stitch on your sewing machine, or hand embroider a stem stitch.

Decorative Stitches

Instead of a straight stitch, you may want to use a decorative stitch on your sewing machine. I tried a few different decorative stitches on a piece of scrap, adjusting the length and width of the stitches until I found one that looked like a stem stitch (at least from a distance!). If you want the line details to show up, you may want to use a slightly darker thread color. For instance, I used gold thread on the yellow roses.

3. Make 32 appliquéd blocks. Gently press and then trim each block to 8½" x 8½", referring to "Squaring Up Blocks" on page 41.

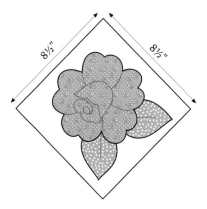

8½"   8½"

Make 32.

ASSEMBLING THE QUILT TOP

1. Mark a diagonal line from corner to corner on each 4½" cream square. Place a marked square on the corner of a yellow quarter-square triangle, right sides together and raw edges aligned. Sew along the marked line and trim away the corner fabric, leaving a ¼" seam allowance. Press the seam allowances toward the yellow. Make 14 side setting triangles.

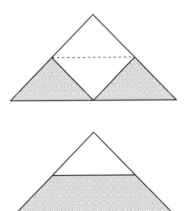

Make 14.

Bonus Triangle Squares

This little trick is so simple; I wish I'd thought of it. Luckily someone else did! After marking the diagonal line on the 4½" cream square, draw a second line ½" from the first line. Sew along both marked lines, and then cut between the two stitched lines. You'll have a setting triangle for this quilt and a bonus triangle square for another project.

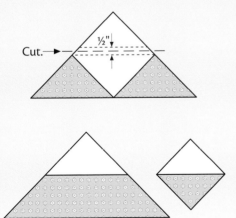

2. Lay out the blocks, setting triangles, and corner triangles in diagonal rows as shown in the quilt layout diagram. When you're satisfied with the arrangement, sew the pieces in each row together. Press the seam allowances in opposite directions from one row to the next. Sew the rows together and press the seam allowances in one direction. Add the corner triangles last. Note that the setting triangles are a bit oversized and will be trimmed in the next step.

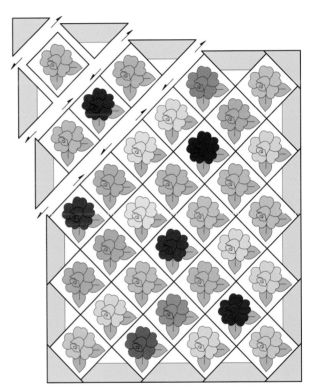

Quilt layout

3. To trim and straighten the quilt top, align the ¼"
   line on your ruler with the outermost points of the
   appliquéd blocks. Use a rotary cutter to trim any
   excess fabric, leaving a ¼" seam allowance. Square
   the corners of the quilt top as necessary.

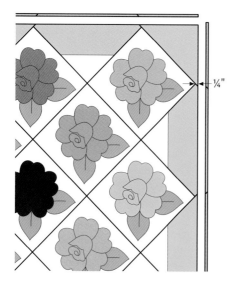

4. Sew the 1¾"-wide cream inner-border strips
   together end to end. Referring to "Borders" on page
   12, measure the length of the quilt top; trim two
   cream strips to this length and sew them to the
   sides of the quilt top. Press the seam allowances
   toward the border. Measure the width of the quilt
   top; trim two cream strips to this length and sew
   them to the top and bottom of the quilt. Press the
   seam allowances toward the border.

5. Sew the 3½"-wide mint green middle-border strips
   together end to end. Measure, cut, and sew the
   strips to the sides, and then the top and bottom of
   the quilt for the middle border, pressing as shown.
   In the same manner, sew the 2½"-wide pink outer-
   border strips end to end, and then measure, cut, and

sew the strips to the quilt top for the outer border,
pressing as shown.

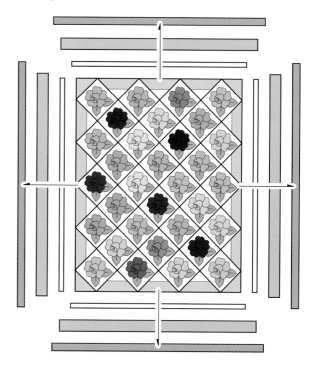

FINISHING

Cut and piece the backing fabric, and then layer the
quilt top with batting and backing. After basting the
layers together, hand or machine quilt as desired; see
the quilting suggestion below. Trim the batting and
backing so the edges are even with the quilt top. Using
the 2"-wide pink strips, make and attach binding.

Quilting Suggestion

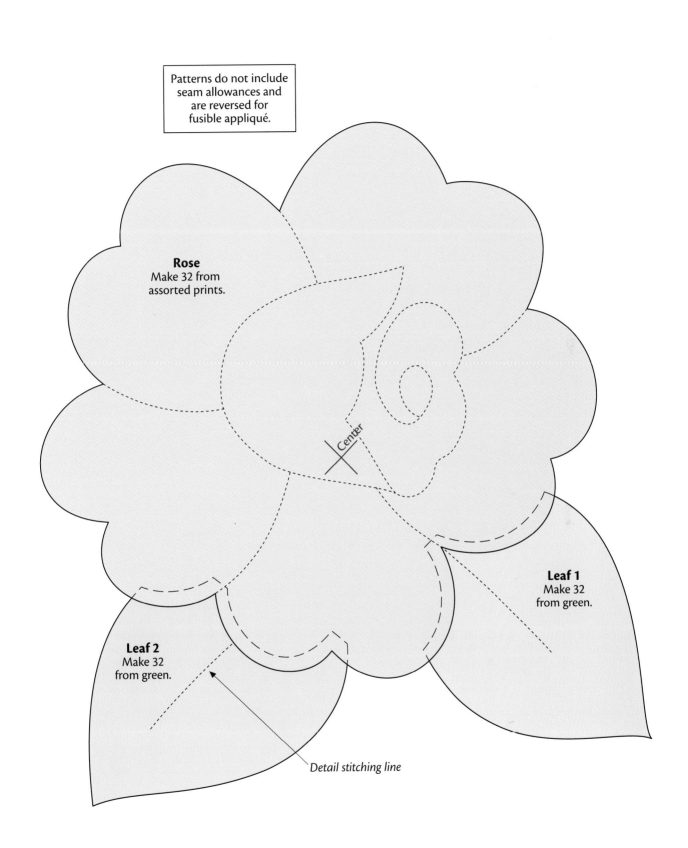

Patterns do not include
seam allowances and
are reversed for
fusible appliqué.

Rose
Make 32 from
assorted prints.

Center

Leaf 1
Make 32
from green.

Leaf 2
Make 32
from green.

Detail stitching line

Bride's Quilt

Finished Quilt Size: 60½" x 60½"

Finished Block Size: 11"

Pieced, appliquéd, and machine quilted by Nancy Mahoney

This wonderful block from Laura Wheeler Designs was available from the Needlecraft Department of the *Des Moines Tribune*. Postage on the original envelope is 1¢ which dates the pattern to 1930 or before. This block was designed for piecing, but if the partially pieced block that was found in the envelope is any indication, only an experienced quilter would attempt this block. Perhaps that's why it's hard to find this pattern made into a quilt! But, I really liked the block and knew there had to be a simpler way. So I omitted a few lines, switched the templates to appliqué and . . . voilà! Golden rings, hearts, and a pink ribbon in the border make this a perfect gift for any bride—young or old.

Dateline–1938

* DuPont promotes its first nylon product—a toothbrush

* Howard Hughes flies around the world in a record time of 3 days, 19 hours

* First issue of *Action Comics* with Superman on the cover is released

* Orson Welles's radio adaptation of *The War of the Worlds* is broadcast, causing mass panic in the eastern United States

* Kate Smith sings a rendition of Irvin Berlin's "God Bless America" for the first time on radio during an Armistice Day broadcast

* Books released include *Rebecca* by Daphne du Maurier and *The Yearling* by Marjorie Kinnan Rawlings

* *Snow White and the Seven Dwarfs* is released to theaters and becomes the biggest grossing film of the decade

* Academy Award winner for Best Picture of 1938 is *You Can't Take It with You*, starring James Stewart

MATERIALS

Yardages are based on 42"-wide fabrics.
Fat eighths measure 9" x 21".

4 yards of cream solid fabric for blocks and outer border

1¼ yards of pink 1930s reproduction print for inner border, border appliqués, and binding

64 squares, 4" x 4", **or** 1 yard *total* of assorted 1930s reproduction prints for heart appliqués

8 fat eighths of assorted pink 1930s reproduction prints for blocks and appliqués

⅜ yard *each* of 2 yellow 1930s reproduction prints for ring appliqués

4 yards of backing fabric

66" x 66" piece of batting

Heat-resistant template plastic

Appliqué Technique

This quilt was made with a starch appliqué method; however if you prefer, you can use the "Fusible Appliqué" method described on page 10. You'll need 4¼ yards of 16"-wide fusible web.

CUTTING

From the *lengthwise* grain of the cream solid fabric, cut:

2 outer-border strips, 7½" x 64"

2 outer-border strips, 7½" x 50"

From the remaining cream solid fabric, cut:

16 squares, 11½" x 11½"

From *each* of the 8 assorted pink prints, cut:

8 squares, 3¼" x 3¼" (64 total)

2 squares, 2½" x 2½" (16 total)

From *each* of the 2 yellow prints, cut:

4 strips, 2¾" x 42" (8 total)

From the pink print, cut:

7 strips, 2½" x 42"; crosscut into 24 squares, 2½" x 2½"

7 binding strips, 2" x 42"

5 inner-border strips, 1½" x 42"

MAKING THE BLOCKS

Refer to "Starch Appliqué" on page 8 and use the patterns on pages 61 and 62 to make one heat-resistant template of each shape. Refer to "Bonus Triangle Squares" on page 53 to save leftover triangle squares for another project.

1. Draw a diagonal line from corner to corner on the wrong side of each 3¼" pink square. Then position a marked square on diagonally opposite corners of each cream square, right sides together. Sew along the marked line and trim away the excess fabric, leaving a ¼" seam allowance. In the same manner, sew pink squares to the remaining two corners of each cream square to complete 16 background blocks. Set aside the trimmed triangles for another project.

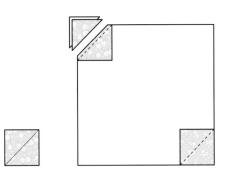

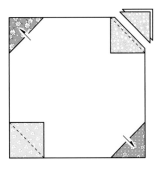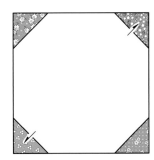

Make 16.

2. Sew two different yellow strips together along their long edges as shown. Press the seam allowances open. Make four of these strips sets.

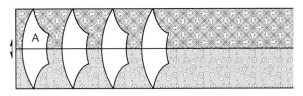

Make 4 strip sets.
Cut 64 pieces.

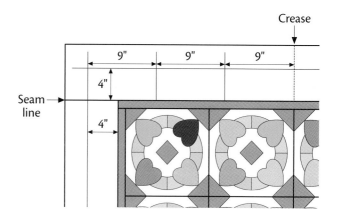

3. Fold each background block in half horizontally and vertically and finger-press to establish centering lines. Using the strip sets from step 2, prepare and appliqué four A pieces to a background block, referring to the pattern and photo on page 56 as needed for placement guidance. Make 16.

4. Using the assorted prints, prepare and appliqué four hearts (B) to the background block, again referring to the pattern for placement guidance. Then using the 2½" pink squares, prepare and appliqué a C square in the center of the block. Make 16 appliquéd blocks.

Make 16.

ASSEMBLING THE QUILT TOP

1. Lay out four rows of four blocks each as shown. Sew the blocks together in rows, pressing the seam allowances in opposite directions from one row to the next. Sew the rows together and press the seam allowances in one direction.

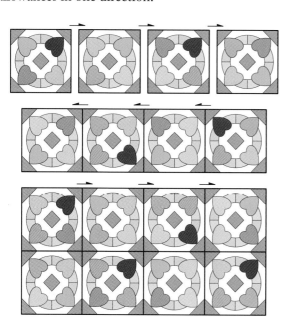

2. Sew the 1½"-wide pink inner-border strips together end to end. From this strip, cut two 44½"-long strips and sew them to opposite sides of the quilt top. Then cut two 46½"-long strips and sew them to the top and bottom of the quilt top. Press the seam allowances toward the just-added borders. The quilt top should measure 46½" square for the appliquéd border to fit properly.

3. Referring to "Borders" on page 12, measure the length of the quilt top; it should be 46½". Trim the two shorter cream outer-border strips to this length and sew them to the sides of the quilt top. Press the seam allowances toward the pink border. Measure the width of the quilt top; it should be 60½". Trim the two remaining cream outer-border strips to this length and sew them to the top and bottom of the quilt in the same manner.

ADDING THE APPLIQUÉ BORDER

1. Fold each cream border in half and finger-press to establish centering creases. Using an erasable or water-soluble marker, draw a line 4" from the border seam lines as shown. For placement of the C squares, measure 9" from the center crease and draw a line. Then measure 9" from the drawn line and draw a second line.

2. Refer to "Starch Appliqué" on page 8. Use the remaining 2½" pink squares to prepare 24 C squares and the remaining pink fabric to prepare 24 D pieces. Position the C and D pieces on the cream border, centering the pieces on the marked lines and referring to the photo on page 56 and the layout diagram for placement guidance. Appliqué the pieces in place.

FINISHING

Cut and piece the backing fabric, and then layer the quilt top with batting and backing. After basting the layers together, hand or machine quilt as desired; see the quilting suggestion below. Trim the batting and backing so the edges are even with the quilt top. Using the 2"-wide pink binding strips, make and attach binding.

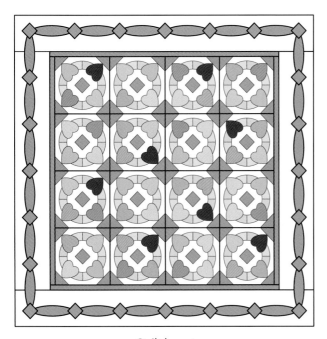

Quilt layout

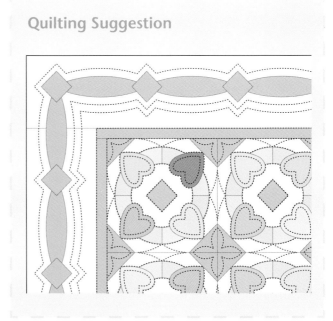

Quilting Suggestion

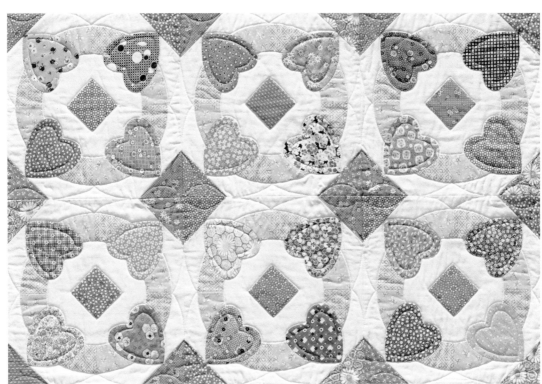

B
Make 64.

A
Make 64.

Place on seam line.

Patterns do not include
seam allowances.

C
Make 40.

Center

Pattern does not include
seam allowance.
Add ³⁄₁₆" seam allowance
along the curved edges
if you plan to use
starch appliqué.

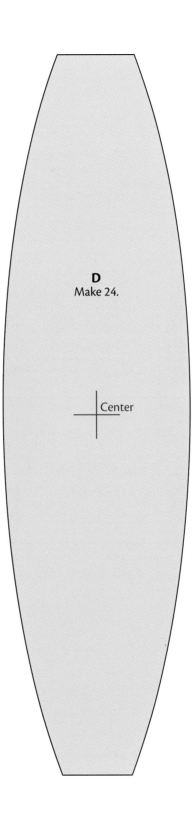

D
Make 24.

— Center

About the Author

Author, teacher, fabric designer, and award-winning quiltmaker, Nancy Mahoney has enjoyed making quilts for more than 20 years. An impressive range of her beautiful quilts have been featured in many national and international quilt magazines.

This is Nancy's tenth book with Martingale & Company. Her other best-selling books include, *Ribbon Star Quilts* (2008), *Appliqué Quilt Revival* (2008), and *Quilt Revival* (2006).

Almost entirely self taught, Nancy continues to explore new ways to combine traditional blocks and updated techniques to create quilts that are fun and easy to make.

Nancy lives in Florida with her life partner of over 30 years, Tom, and their umbrella cockatoo, Prince.

There's More Online!

Visit www.nancymahoney.com for more great patterns plus details about Nancy's fabric line and class offerings. Find books on quilting and more at www.martingale-pub.com.

Dateline–1939

* Regular television broadcasts begin in the United States

* The World's Fair opens in New York City and includes the first exhibitions of television

* Books released include *The Grapes of Wrath* by John Steinbeck and *The Wild Palms* by William Faulkner

* Songs released include "Over the Rainbow," sung by Judy Garland, and "Jim Jam Jump," sung by Ella Fitzgerald

* Batman comics appear for the first time

* Popular films are *The Wizard of Oz*, *Stagecoach*, and *Of Mice and Men*

* *Gone with the Wind* wins 10 Academy Awards, including Best Picture of 1939

You might also enjoy these other fine titles from

Martingale & Company

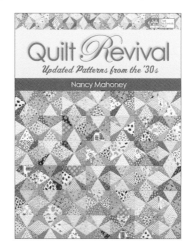

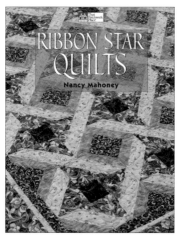

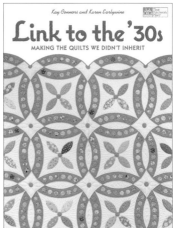

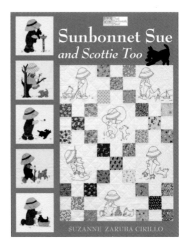

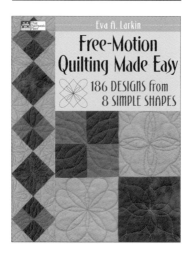

Our books are available at bookstores and your favorite craft, fabric, and yarn retailers.
Visit us at www.martingale-pub.com or contact us at:

That Patchwork Place®

America's Best-Loved Quilt Books®

Martingale®
& COMPANY

America's Best-Loved Craft & Hobby Books®
America's Best-Loved Knitting Books®

1-800-426-3126
International: 1-425-483-3313
Fax: 1-425-486-7596
Email: info@martingale-pub.com